THE
QUICK-START
GUIDE
TO THE WHOLE
BIBLE

Books by Dr. William H. Marty

FROM BETHANY HOUSE PUBLISHERS

The Jesus Story
The Whole Bible Story
The World of Jesus
*The Quick-Start Guide to the Whole Bible**

Books by Dr. Boyd Seevers

Warfare in the Old Testament: The Organization,
Weapons, and Tactics of Ancient Near Eastern Armies

FROM BETHANY HOUSE PUBLISHERS

Hidden in Plain Sight
*The Quick-Start Guide to the Whole Bible***

*with Dr. Boyd Seevers
**with Dr. William H. Marty

THE QUICK-START GUIDE TO THE WHOLE BIBLE

Understanding the Big Picture Book-by-Book

Dr. William H. Marty
and Dr. Boyd Seevers

BETHANY HOUSE PUBLISHERS

a division of Baker Publishing Group
Minneapolis, Minnesota

© 2014 by William H. Marty and Boyd V. Seevers

Published by Bethany House Publishers
11400 Hampshire Avenue South
Bloomington, Minnesota 55438
www.bethanyhouse.com

Bethany House Publishers is a division of
Baker Publishing Group, Grand Rapids, Michigan

Printed in the United States of America

Library of Congress Cataloging-in-Publication Data
Marty, William Henry, author.
    The quick start guide to the whole Bible : understanding the big picture book-by-book / Dr. William H. Marty, Dr. Boyd Seevers.
        pages cm
    Summary: "Two professors offer a compact reference guide to the whole Bible, with helpful book-by-book summaries as well as application for what it means to the reader"— Provided by publisher.
    ISBN 978-0-7642-1128-7 (pbk. : alk. paper))
    1. Bible—Introductions. I. Seevers, Boyd, author. II. Title.
BS475.3.M375 2014
220.6′1—dc23   2014006610

Cover design by Gearbox

14 15 16 17 18 19 20   7 6 5 4 3 2

Contents

New Testament

Introduction

Is This Book for Me?

Perhaps you're a fairly new follower of Christ and would like some help with the big picture of what's really going on in the Bible. Or perhaps you've gone to church for many years but find that you still don't understand some books of the Bible very well. (Join the club!) Or perhaps you enjoy reading the Bible but don't own a collection of Bible reference books, and you'd like a simple and affordable book that can help you understand what's in the Bible and what it means. If any of these circumstances describes you, then you're very likely to benefit from *The Quick-Start Guide to the Whole Bible*.

How Will This Book Help Me Better Understand the Bible?

The Quick-Start Guide to the Whole Bible was written by respected Bible professors who have been honored as outstanding teachers by their respective institutions for their ability to explain God's Word. Dr. Boyd Seevers of University of Northwestern–St. Paul wrote the Old Testament chapters, and Dr. William H. Marty of Moody Bible Institute wrote the New Testament chapters. Now they're sharing their knowledge and insights, and in this book they'll take you through the Bible one book at a time to explain three aspects simply and clearly.

First, they'll help you understand what's important about the setting or background for each book. When we try to understand a book that's come to us from a time, place, and culture very different from our own, it usually helps to begin by familiarizing ourselves with the original situation. Thus, each chapter will begin by addressing questions like: "Who wrote this book?" "To whom was he writing?" "What did he write?" "Where did the events occur?" "Why was he writing this material to these people?"

Second, they'll summarize the content of each book as plainly and efficiently as possible. This will help answer the question "What is this book of the Bible *saying*?"

Third, after looking at the background and summarizing the content, they'll explain each book's significance. This should help answer the question "What does this book *mean*?" In doing so, they will examine the book's importance both for the original audience and also for believers like us today.

Old Testament

Dedication

This book's Old Testament section is dedicated to the students at the University of Northwestern–St. Paul who have filled the honors sections of Old Testament Survey. It is an ongoing pleasure to discuss with them the challenges of understanding and applying the Old Testament. The first half of this book is one of the fruits of those discussions.

Acknowledgments

The author of the Old Testament section wishes to thank the following:

My very capable and kind editor, Andy McGuire, as well as the rest of the friendly and professional staff at Bethany House. Working with them is a pleasure.

Friend and former student Sarah Schock, for her skilled work editing these chapters. Also my other student editors: David Detloff, Aubree Else, Kelsey Richards, Kristine Sollie, Christine Stevens, and Wade Weeldreyer, for their enthusiastic work and helpful suggestions.

Genesis

Setting

The book of Genesis does not name its author, but elsewhere (Exodus 17:14; Mark 7:10) the Bible implies that Moses at least wrote much of the first five books of the Old Testament (also known as the Pentateuch), including Genesis. Moses would have initially written these five books for the Israelites who had come out of Egypt with him.

In Genesis, Moses explains to these Israelites the origins of the world, of human beings, of sin, of the Israelite people and their first covenant with God. Whereas contemporary readers may look to the first part of Genesis for answers to questions that are important in modern thought (such as how and when the world began), Moses likely addressed questions more applicable to his original audience: "How many gods are there?" "Is our God like the gods of the peoples around us?" "How should we relate to God?" Genesis can best be understood as answering queries like these, although how it addresses them continues to tell believers throughout time what God is like and how we can walk with him.

Summary

The author begins with the creation story (Genesis 1:1–2:3), then divides the rest of the book into ten sections, each beginning with the phrase "This is the account of" or "This is the written account of" (2:4; 5:1, etc.). However, many readers today find it helpful to understand Genesis in two major parts: Primeval History (1–11), telling of the world's earliest history, and then Patriarchal History (12–50), which tells about the Israelite patriarchs Abraham, Isaac, and Jacob, and of Jacob's twelve sons.

Primeval History

In chapters 1 through 11, God creates and guides the whole world in order to bless it. This section includes events such as the creation, the fall of humanity, the flood in the time of Noah, and the Tower of Babel (e.g., see Matthew 24:37; Romans 5:14).

These earliest chapters also give rise to some of the most vexing questions that someone today might ask of the Bible: "When did creation take place?" "Did God create everything in seven twenty-four-hour days?" "How could human lifespans have been so long prior to the flood?" (e.g., Genesis 5:1–32). "Who were the 'sons of God' and the 'daughters of humans?'" (6:2). The original author and his audience probably knew the answers to such questions, but modern readers struggle to find the answers in the text.

The book begins with the story of creation—a grand, beautifully crafted account of God taking a dark, chaotic void (1:2) and reshaping it into an orderly masterpiece filled with light and life. God then rests, symbolizing that his work is complete, an act the Israelites later were to emulate: One day of every week they would rest as a sign of their national covenant with him (Exodus 31:13).

The text then shifts in Genesis chapters 2 through 3 to a narrative of events in one part of creation, called the garden of Eden. God graciously gives to the first man food, work, and dominion over the animal realm. Despite his marvelous situation, the man God made is incomplete until God also creates the woman—the man's ideal counterpart—and together they represent God's perfect pattern for marriage.

Tragically, their wholeness is forever broken through the deception of the serpent, who entices them to disobey God's clear command. God rightly judges all the guilty parties. He likewise graciously provides for the people's immediate needs and for the continuation of human life, though because of the entrance of sin, all must face the specter of death.

Sin's worsening effects are demonstrated in the stories that follow. Adam and Eve's son Cain first responds poorly to God's rebuke for an earlier choice and then murders Abel, his brother. Cain's line of descendants is underscored by the proud and violent Lamech, and humankind's prospects look bleak. By contrast, the birth of Cain's brother Seth offers hope, as people then began "to call on the name of the LORD" (4:26), which seems to be a description of proper worship of the one true God.

The subsequent genealogy, in chapter 5, serves several purposes. It connects the book's first two major characters, Adam and Noah; it demonstrates that the fall indeed led to death for (almost) all humans; and it highlights Enoch, who walked with God (one of the book's primary emphases) and did not face death.

Like the fall, the subsequent story of the flood provides another example of sin, judgment, and a new beginning. Whatever the identity of the "sons of God" (6:2, 4—fallen angels? wicked rulers? godly descendants of Seth corrupted by marrying descendants of Cain?), their sin leads to God's judgment on humanity. He chooses Noah, a righteous man, to rescue a human remnant from destruction. Like in the story of the creation, watery chaos again covers the earth. And again, from watery chaos come land, plants, animals, and humans. In yet another parallel, Noah sins, demonstrating that sin has not been eradicated from the re-created world.

The Primeval History concludes with God's dispersal of arrogant and rebellious humanity at the Tower of Babel—another act of judgment that precedes a shift in God's program for the world.

Patriarchal History

The account in chapters 12 through 50 follows the lives of Abraham and three generations of his descendants. With Abraham, the book's focus narrows from God working with the entire world to one family, through whom God intends to bless the whole world.

God calls Abraham (originally Abram) to leave the support and familiarity of his home. Abraham immediately obeys, despite the cost and risk, and migrates to Canaan. This would one day be the homeland for his descendants—the book's original audience.

Abraham lives most of the rest of his life in Canaan. When he makes an unfortunate detour to Egypt, God protects and enriches him and his clan. Later God formalizes his promises to Abraham (and his future descendants) in a covenantal ceremony, guaranteeing land, offspring, and blessing to his line. But Sarah is barren, so she gives her servant, Hagar, to her husband, as a surrogate, and Ishmael is born. Later God repeats his promise and provides Isaac, the heir, through Sarah. Abraham's story culminates with the account of his willingness to sacrifice his beloved son, showing plainly the kind of trusting and obedient follower that God seeks.

The line of promise continues with Isaac and moves on to Isaac's son Jacob. One detail not to miss: In each of these first three generations, God overcomes a wife's barrenness (Sarah's, Rebekah's, and Rachel's) to miraculously continue the line. Further, Jacob becomes the heir of promise despite being the second born. Unfortunately, Isaac's younger son repeatedly demonstrates his flawed character, especially in his penchant to deceive in order to get what he wants. Jacob's deception of his father leads to great family conflict and his own exile.

Later Laban, Jacob's father-in-law, turns the tables and deceives Jacob. As a result, Jacob ends up with both of Laban's daughters (Leah and Rachel) as his wives. Ultimately Jacob has twelve sons—the ancestors of the later Israelite tribes. Still, through God's unconditional promises to Abraham, Jacob is blessed with family and wealth, as well as the name *Israel,* and he returns to Canaan.

The Patriarchal History concludes with chapters 37 through 50, stories of Jacob's sons that focus primarily on Joseph, the gifted son of Jacob's favored wife, Rachel. Joseph's ability to interpret dreams demonstrates that God has chosen him for greatness. God's favor doesn't protect him from mistreatment at the hands of his envious brothers or of his later Egyptian master. In Egypt, Joseph suffers unjustly as a slave and prisoner for thirteen years, but his abilities and his character prepare him for his unexpected dramatic promotion to become Pharaoh's chief advisor, second-in-command over all Egypt.

Joseph eventually meets his brothers, but he doesn't immediately reveal his identity. He first tests them, apparently to learn if they regret their earlier sins against him and are now able to accept the favoritism Joseph shows toward his brother Benjamin (Rachel's other son). Their responses, combined with Joseph's willingness to forgive, enable a beautiful and complete reconciliation.

The brothers had come from Canaan to Egypt because of a severe famine. Because of Joseph, Jacob and the rest of the Abraham-descended clan now move to Egypt in what is initially a blessing. In time, this blessing becomes a bondage from which God will rescue the clan-become-nation, at the time of Moses and the exodus.

Significance

What does Genesis teach? In other words, what do God and the human author mean to convey through these accounts of the beginnings of the world and of his covenant people?

- -

Israel's God Is Different From the Other "Gods"

First, this book of origins tells the early Israelites that their God is nothing like the gods of the nations around them. Others worship pagan gods with humanlike faults, who supposedly had created the world through chaos, deception, and violence. By contrast, the God of Israel creates with purpose, power, and splendor. At the time of Moses, this magnificent God would invite the Israelites to join with him in covenant—an invitation surely meriting their obedience.

Obedience Brings Blessing; Disobedience Brings Judgment

Second, Genesis shows that God creates a beautiful, orderly world, full of life and good things, including humans. He yearns to bless it, but human disobedience brings death and corruption—not only to humanity but also to every aspect of the creation—blunting the effects of God's blessing.

Human disobedience continues after the fall, and God repeatedly has to withhold his blessing and judge the guilty: Adam and Eve, Cain, the rest of humanity at the time of Noah, and all humanity at the Tower of Babel. Though God would bless the line of Abraham, the failures of faith and the disobedience in each generation of the patriarchs caused both short- and long-term consequences for the guilty individuals as well as for those around them—and sometimes well beyond.

But people are also capable of great acts of faith and obedience, and God uses those who trust and follow him. As illustrated by Seth, Enoch, Noah, especially Abraham, and finally Joseph, these men became channels of God's blessing to themselves and others. Later the Israelites, the original audience of Genesis, would face the same choice: turn from God, disobey his word, and merit his judgment (as they often did), or believe God, obey his commands (as they sometimes did), and receive his blessing.

God's people today also face the choice to obey and be blessed or disobey and be judged. Though we live in a very different world from Adam, Abraham, or Moses, God still searches for those who will trust what he says and do what he asks. If we choose to believe and obey, we will know blessing and a fruitful life.

God Controls Human Life and World History

Third, though Genesis shows that human choices have a profound impact on the world, the book likewise clearly demonstrates that God directs both human life and world history. Creation submitted to God's sovereignty as he created by his Word. God's subsequent acts of judgment also reflect his control—the one who made the world has the power and authority to break and remake it as he sees fit.

God also controls life. He gave humans life and everything they needed for life; when they chose instead to reject him, his judgment for their sin was death. He separated the farmer from his land when judging Cain, and he scattered people by confusing their languages at the Tower of Babel. In the patriarchal stories, he promised offspring to those who had none and repeatedly enabled the barren to give birth. Though God always worked in concert with the choices people made, he also directed how their lives would play out despite famine, war, hostile enemies, and evil rulers.

God also controls the course of history. He began it at creation, nearly ended it at the flood, and then started a special nation (Israel) through a barren, elderly couple. This special nation would have a miraculous history, as illustrated both in the family stories of Genesis and in the deliverance through the exodus of the book's original audience.

God, through Moses, taught the book's original audience that they had an awesome God who is in charge of the world and would bless them if they trusted and obeyed him. The world of Genesis has changed, but the message remains the same.

Exodus

Setting

Exodus describes the acts and character of Israel's God at the birth of Israel as a nation. The book clearly points to Israel's leader, Moses, as its general author (17:14; 24:4). Later biblical characters, including Jesus, also refer to information in Exodus as written by Moses (e.g., Mark 7:10). This great leader wrote Exodus to record the monumental event that helped birth the nation—the deliverance of God's people from slavery in Egypt (chapters 1–18)—and the defining national covenant between God and Israel (19–24). It also describes the construction of the tabernacle, where God would meet with them (25–40).

Moses recorded these events so that the Israelites of his day (c. fifteenth or thirteenth century BC), as well as those living throughout the rest of the Old Testament era, would better know what their great, delivering God was like and how they should relate to him. And although more than three thousand years have passed since Moses led Israel out of Egypt, believers today still marvel at and learn from God's might and character reflected in these accounts.

Summary

Exodus neatly divides into two main parts—the account of God delivering the Israelites from bondage (1–18) and a record of the covenant he made with them (19–40). The second section includes a description of the tabernacle, the covenantal meeting place at that time between God and his people.

The Deliverance

Chapters 1 through 18 describe how God delivers the Israelites after several hundreds of years in Egypt. Moving there during the time of Joseph's power (recorded at the close of Genesis) saves Abraham's descendants from starvation, but the passage of centuries and their subjection to slavery, under a new ruler, leads the Israelites to cry out to God for release. Their patient and faithful God raises up a deliverer in Moses, who survives Pharaoh's early threat on his life through the bravery of his parents and the kind actions of one of Pharaoh's daughters. When he grows to adulthood, Moses tries to help his people, yet ends up fleeing for his life and spending the next four decades in exile, working as a lowly shepherd.

God then calls Moses to free his people from the mighty kingdom of Egypt. Having been raised in the palace, Moses no doubt understood how unlikely such an outcome would be, and this probably caused his reluctance to follow God's calling (contrast Abraham's response to God's call in Genesis 12). Even so, Moses eventually obeys, returns to Egypt, and with help from his brother Aaron, demands that Pharaoh release the Israelites.

A proud ruler of a great nation does not take kindly to orders from shepherds (which Moses had become). When Pharaoh repeatedly refuses to acknowledge God and release the people from bondage, God uses powerful plagues to bring disaster on Egypt's land, economy, and people to break the pharaoh's will. After he finally relents and agrees to free the Israelites, he quickly reverses course and pursues with his chariots—the core of the era's greatest military. A throng of slaves stands no chance against such a force, except that their God miraculously shapes their deliverance and the destruction of their foes through the parting and the closing of the Red Sea.

The God who had given the Israelites freedom then provides food and water in the desert as they make their way toward Mount Sinai. There they meet with their awesome God and bind themselves to him in covenant.

The Covenant

The covenant God makes with the Israelites is similar in form to international treaties of the time. God pledges to protect and bless them *if* they will worship him alone and faithfully follow his commandments. God spells out his expectations in the form of commands both general (the Ten Commandments) and specific (case laws showing how to apply this law code to particular situations). Moses and the nation's other leaders ratify the pact on behalf of the people, and Israel is henceforth bound to this covenant (known as the Mosaic covenant) that will shape the course of their national history.

The Covenantal Meeting Place

When Moses ascended Mount Sinai to receive the covenant from God, he also received plans for the tabernacle, where God would meet with his people. This portable shrine includes a courtyard with installations for sacrificing animals and for washing—to facilitate the symbolic removal of the people's sins. In the courtyard stands a portable building consisting of two rooms—first, the holy place, in which priests conduct specific daily rituals, and second, the most holy place (or Holy of Holies), which houses the ark of the covenant, a sacred symbol of the faith. In the most holy place, only the high priest may carry out a ritual, and only once a year.

The Israelites immediately turn from God and construct a golden calf (an idol to worship), falling under God's punishment. Then, recommitting to their covenant, they build the tabernacle as specified, establishing the place where a sinful but sanctified people can meet with their holy God.

Significance

Israel's God Is Faithful

Along with recording what God did at the time of the exodus (he had freed them, protected them, provided for them, and more), this book also reveals what God is like. Centuries earlier, God swore to Abraham that his descendants (the Israelites) would be numerous; they would live in an oppressive land for four hundred years, and then he would release them and give them the land of Canaan as their own. No matter how unlikely these events may have seemed, the book of Exodus shows that by the time of Moses, God had faithfully fulfilled his promises, and surely he would give them the Promised Land as well. Though from a human vantage point it seemed God had taken a very long time, he is faithful and will always fulfill what he has promised.

Israel's God Is Powerful

Second, Exodus shows the power of Israel's God—multiplying a people, rescuing and empowering Moses, striking their mighty oppressor with even mightier plagues, defeating its military, providing all needed sustenance in the desert, and unforgettably revealing himself at Mount Sinai through thunder, lightning, smoke, and fire. Surely the God who could do all of this for his people had the power necessary to do the rest of what he'd promised: help them survive the desert, arrive at Canaan, and conquer it.

Israel's God Is Willing to Bind Himself to His People in Covenant

This faithful, powerful God also formally binds himself to the Israelites in the covenant formed at Mount Sinai. Scholars often call this agreement the Mosaic covenant, after the leader who represented Israel during the covenant-making process. When God first called Moses at the burning bush, he revealed his covenantal name— YHWH (in our Bibles this is often rendered "Lord"), derived from the verb *to be,* and apparently a reference to his self-existence (i.e., "I AM" [*YHWH,* or *Yahweh*]). After freeing his people, God uses that event as his self-identification in the establishment of the covenant (Exodus 20:2), in which the Sovereign of the world commits to provide for and protect his covenantal partners—the Israelites—if they will faithfully obey and worship him alone.

While Christians today relate to God through the new covenant Jesus established rather than the Mosaic covenant established here, we as well have the privilege of relating to the God who loves us and created us to love and serve him.

Leviticus

Setting

Leviticus forms a natural sequel to the book of Exodus, since it explains several aspects of religious life the Israelites were to practice at the tabernacle they built (recorded at the end of Exodus). God gave these instructions during the year the Israelites were camped at Mount Sinai following their deliverance from Egypt (c. fifteenth or thirteenth century BC), and Moses apparently recorded them shortly thereafter.

Leviticus describes the sacrifices the Israelites were to make at the tabernacle, the priests who were to officiate those offerings, various laws pertaining to ritual purity, and the holidays included in the Hebrew calendar. Although many aspects of this religious system were later replaced with the new covenant following the life and ministry of Jesus, Leviticus includes several important principles that apply to God's people in any age. Foremost among these is that God is holy and his people are to reflect that holiness.

Summary

The concept of holiness dominates Leviticus—the holy God of Israel desires that his people be holy as well. Chapters 1–10 describe how they were to practice holiness in their religious system, and chapters 11–27 explain how they should incorporate holiness into their daily lives.

Holiness in Worship

The first seven chapters describe in detail the five main offerings the Israelites were to present to God in various conditions of life. The next three chapters record the selection of Aaron and his descendants to serve as priests, including the deaths of two of his sons who acted contrary to what God required (compare the nation's similar failure with the golden calf in Exodus 32–33).

Holiness in Daily Life

The rest of the book details how the Israelites were to reflect holiness in daily life. God gave laws that guided them to maintain ritual purity in matters such as proper (vs. improper) food, sexual boundaries, and social laws. God also instituted eight holidays they were to celebrate, either to commemorate God's past redemptive acts or to celebrate harvests in the annual agricultural cycle. These descriptions provided vital information for the worshipers of the time and the priests who officiated the sacrificial ceremonies.

Significance

What is holiness? In this context, first, holiness meant *separation* from what was common or normal. Their holy God was separate from his creation. Israel, the priests, the Sabbath, and all items associated with divine worship were separated from the common people and common uses, and so considered holy. Leviticus gives guidelines for the people on the matters that were to be holy by virtue of separation.

Leviticus also addresses the second aspect of holiness, which is *purity of character*. Israel's God clearly had purity of character (unlike the gods of the surrounding peoples), and he desired that his people reflect his purity. Under the system he prescribed for them, blood sacrifices would symbolically cover their sins and *make* them pure. When the Israelites carried out the sacrifices prescribed in Leviticus with a trusting heart, their current sins were atoned for (or covered)—any future sins would require further sacrifices. In addition, they needed to obey God's instructions for daily life in order to *maintain* the purity accomplished by proper sacrifice and faith.

Although the new covenant provides the ultimate sacrifice (the blood of Jesus) that never needs repeating, and many of the ancient rules for holy living have changed, God's desire that his people reflect his holiness has not changed. "Be holy because I, the LORD your God, am holy" (Leviticus 19:2). Christians today should separate themselves from all ungodly, worldly influence and reflect God's pure character.

Numbers

Setting

This book continues the history of the Israelite people. In Genesis, God promised Abraham innumerable descendants to whom he would give the land of Canaan. God began this line with the faithful and obedient Abraham living in Canaan, declaring that his descendants would leave (when Jacob's clan moved to Egypt) and then, after several centuries, return as a multitude. By the time of the exodus, that people had indeed become numerous; God delivered them from Egypt so they could begin their trek across the wilderness of Sinai toward their Promised Land. When they stopped at Mount Sinai, they made a covenant with God that formalized their religious system and laid out the guidelines to which they were obligated (history and details are recorded in Exodus and Leviticus).

Numbers describes the continuation of the journey toward Canaan as well as the nation's failures and successes in keeping their covenant. Their leader, Moses, wrote this book at the end of their sojourn, as they were at the border of Canaan. Forty years had passed since their parents had left Egypt; persistent lack of faith and repeated failure to obey God had cost the lives of an entire generation. The book of Numbers details what happened during those years, in part to warn the second generation (and all of God's future people) of the terrible consequences of unbelief and rebellion.

Summary

Numbers begins after the people's mass departure from Egypt, with the initial generation of Israelites camped at Mount Sinai. It ends thirty-eight years later with the second generation camped just outside Canaan. As the book opens, the nation is making preparations at Mount Sinai (1:1–10:10). Next, they travel about one hundred fifty miles to the oasis of Kadesh Barnea, south of Canaan. From there, representatives of each tribe scout out the land. When the people refuse to invade, God condemns them to die in the wilderness (10:11–20:13); they will not trust him, so only their descendants will enter the land.

The first generation passes away as the nation eventually makes its way to a site in the Transjordan, east of the Jordan River and across from the city of Jericho, with the second generation ready to invade (20:14–36:13). The book of Numbers explains why the trip to Canaan took so long, as well as why the first generation could not enjoy the long-anticipated inheritance of its homeland.

Generation One—Failure and Judgment

The book begins at Sinai with the Israelites preparing as one might expect an army readying to begin an invasion. Numbers gets its name from the censuses in chapters 1 and 26, which enumerate for each generation the males twenty-plus years of age (i.e., those eligible to serve as soldiers). The traditional translation of these numbers gives just over six hundred *thousand* adult males, suggesting a total Israelite population (men, women, and children) in

29

excess of two million. The language also allows for a translation of *thousands* as "clans," in which case the total number of males would be about six thousand. Whichever is correct, God has been fulfilling his promise to greatly multiply Abraham's descendants and guide them toward their promised homeland.

After the soldiers are counted, military preparations continue. God prescribes the formations the nation is to use when in camp and on the march. He explains the duties of some clans, and tells how the Israelites should use trumpets to communicate effectively. Also, he gives instructions on matters such as making restitution, presenting offerings, and testing for adultery—instructions that would help the army (and the nation) maintain its ritual purity.

God has given the nation military victories as they've made their way toward Canaan, helping them develop much-needed military skill in the process. Shortly after leaving Egypt (Exodus 17), the Israelites defeated the nomadic Amalekites. Later they won two important battles while traveling northward through the Transjordan, opening up that region for future settlement (Numbers 21).

Unfortunately, their military (and religious) discipline fails as they repeatedly complain and rebel against their commanders—both human (Moses) and divine. God judges the guilty, whether two people or the entire nation, and the guilty die, including Moses' siblings, Miriam and Aaron. God even judges Moses for disobeying a direct command, and the nation's leader is forbidden from entering Canaan. No one is exempt; disobedience carries a high price.

Generation Two—Obedience and Hope

God had to discipline the guilty, and as a result, an entire generation died before Israel would enter Canaan. Nevertheless, God faithfully sustains the people during their forty years in the desert, providing food and water along with other needed guidance for the advancing army and the rest of the migrating nation. The two censuses, taken a generation apart, demonstrate that their numbers remained essentially the same even after all those years in the wilderness.

God not only saves the Israelites from extinction, he also protects them from spiritual attack. When the king of Moab plans to curse them by summoning Balaam, a renowned seer, God makes Balaam bless Israel instead. This enigmatic story shows that God was committed to blessing his people so that they would prosper, even if, for example, it meant co-opting a non-Israelite prophet to do it.

By the end of the book of Numbers, a new generation is in place, ready to move forward with God's plan for the nation. Moses arranges for Joshua to assume leadership, and in both Numbers and Deuteronomy, Moses reviews with the Israelites their history and their covenantal obligations. If this new generation will obey their God, they can learn from their parents' mistakes and move ahead to finally inherit the land that God promised would be given to Abraham's family.

Significance

Numbers describes almost forty years of Israel's history, including a rather dark period. God had freed his people from mighty Egypt, graciously bound himself to them in covenant, and generously supplied for their survival during their lengthy, winding journey. Despite all this, the people still refuse to believe that he will help them conquer Canaan, and disobey his command to begin the conquest. An entire generation then dies in a severe but just punishment.

Despite this failure, God's faithfulness gives Israel hope. He empowers the next generation to win battles that open up lands for settlement as they make their way to the edge of Canaan. Assuming they can learn from past sins, the book ends with the people poised to begin the invasion, committed to trusting God for a successful result.

As Moses did in Numbers, later authors of Scripture also use the failure of the post–exodus generation as a warning about the catastrophic results unbelief and disobedience can yield. Moses would remind the second generation of the sins of their parents and what those decisions had cost them (Deuteronomy 1:19–46). Then, nearly fifteen hundred years later, the apostle Paul notes the failures of that first generation in warning Christians to avoid idolatry, sexual immorality, and even grumbling (1 Corinthians 10:2–12). Although believers today aren't charged with trusting God to invade Canaan, we must trust and obey him in our daily lives in order to inherit all the blessings he desires to give as well as to avoid the painful consequences of unbelief and disobedience.

Deuteronomy

Setting

Deuteronomy acts as a major transition in the Old Testament story of God's people. It brings to a close the five books of the Pentateuch, the story of Israel's forty years in the wilderness, and the life of its great leader Moses. Deuteronomy also sets the stage for Israel's conquest of Canaan and lays out the theological principles that will guide the nation's history for centuries to come.

The book presents a series of speeches by Moses to the second generation of Israelites following the exodus. Apparently he recorded its contents as well (31:9, 24). Of course, the account of his death (chapter 34), was added later. Having left the wilderness of Sinai at last, the people were on the border of Canaan, ready to invade and conquer the land promised to Abraham. In Deuteronomy, Moses both reviews the Israelites' recent past and prepares them for the next phase of their national existence.

Summary

Moses uses historical narrative plus several series of laws to accomplish three tasks: (1) he reviews the preceding four decades, (2) he reiterates the great national covenant between God and Israel, and (3) he leads the new generation to renew that covenant in order to prepare them to successfully conquer and inhabit Canaan.

Moses begins by noting that a journey that should have taken little more than eleven days ended up taking almost forty years (1:2–3). He then summarizes the major events of that journey, when an entire generation perished. They died because they failed to trust that God would keep his word, and they rebelled when they should have begun the invasion. Moses reminds them what happened so that they, and hopefully those who would follow after them, won't likewise rebel.

The national covenant Israel made with their God at Mount Sinai falls into the pattern of most such contracts of the era, as laid out in the book of Deuteronomy:

Preamble—listing the covenantal partners (God and Israel, with Moses as mediator—1:1–5)

Historical Prologue—outlining the historical relationship between the partners (1:6–3:29)

Covenantal Laws—the Ten Commandments, plus specific laws applying to the covenant's general principles in various situations (4–26)

Blessings and Curses—for obedience or disobedience (27–28)

Document Clause—provisions for keeping and periodically reading the covenant (31:9–29)

Witnesses (32)

After repeating the covenant, Moses challenges the second generation to solemnly commit themselves to obeying it. Though the first generation had taken a similar oath, they'd broken it; this generation would have to keep their word in order to inherit the Promised Land.

Significance

Remember—In Order to Act Rightly

Moses wanted this generation of Israelites to know the events from their past as well as to know God's character and actions so that they would obey him and stay true to him. Fifteen times in Deuteronomy Moses commands the people to remember: God delivered them from Egypt; they sinned against him; the content of the covenant they were recommitting to keep. They must *remember*—not only to recall those truths but also to hold to them and act rightly in light of them. God had been faithful to them, and they had failed him; they needed to walk a different path; they needed to keep the "how to" fresh in their minds and hearts.

Obey and Remain Faithful

Moses spells out clearly what the Israelites need to do: worship the one true God alone (6:4); love and follow him with their whole being (6:5); pass that faith on to their children (6:6–9). After God gives them their land, they must remain faithful to God and not follow the gods of the peoples around them. The Ten Commandments and subsequent lists of commands further clarify God's expectations.

Yahweh, Israel's God, was unique among the gods of the ancient Near Eastern peoples. He is sovereign over armies and nations, guiding events to his desired ends. He is gracious and faithful; he is establishing Israel, having preserved them through slavery and a generation in the desert, and is now moving them into their homeland. This God deserves the loyalty of his people.

Christians today relate to God on the basis of the new covenant, established through the finished work of Jesus, rather than through the covenant mediated by Moses at Sinai. This new covenant supersedes the Mosaic covenant (see Hebrews 8:13), and many covenantal statutes Israel was bound to observe are no longer in effect. Some laws carried through from the old covenant to the new (at least nine of the Ten Commandments), but many ritualistic laws did not. Although these other laws may contain principles for guidance in following Jesus, contemporary believers should focus on the commands the New Testament repeats.

Joshua

Setting

The book of Joshua forms a natural transition between the events and themes of the Pentateuch and Israel's subsequent history in its Promised Land. In Genesis, God started with Abraham, promising him innumerable offspring who would one day receive Canaan as their homeland. The rest of Genesis through Deuteronomy follows Abraham's descendants as they move to Egypt, grow in number, gain freedom from bondage, make a covenant with God, and survive forty long years in the desert as they make their way to the edge of the Promised Land. Joshua picks up the story at that point and follows the Israelites into Canaan, where God fulfills his promise to give them the land to settle.

The book is named for its major character, Israel's successor to Moses and leader of the conquest. Joshua himself may have recorded many of the events (8:32; 24:26), but the oft-repeated phrase "to this day" indicates the passing of time, sometimes several centuries from the time of the events to the writing of the book. Regardless, Joshua records God's faithfulness in giving the land to the obedient Israelites. It also serves as a challenge to future generations of God's people to demonstrate similar obedience and loyalty.

Summary

The book is divided into four sections: describing Israel's entrance into Canaan (1–5); the conquest itself (6–12); the division of the land among the tribes (13–21); and Joshua's farewell as their leader (22–24).

The first section describes the invading army entering enemy territory—made more difficult with the Jordan River at flood stage after winter rains. God first promises to be with Joshua, who sends two spies to reconnoiter the city of Jericho, Israel's first objective. Rahab, a local woman, reports that the people are terrified of the invaders and pledges her loyalty to the Israelites and their God.

Reminiscent of his parting of the Red Sea on the flight from Egypt, God stops the Jordan River so the Israelite army can cross on dry ground. Then God tests the faith of the soldiers camped near Jericho by stopping their food supply (manna). They must now eat off of the land, and they are commanded to circumcise themselves (cf. Genesis 34). As he had appeared to Moses at the burning bush, God appears to Joshua and gives him clear but unorthodox instructions for conquering Jericho.

The unusual attack on the city begins Israel's conquest and sets the tone for success, because they obey God. They march around the city for seven days, as ordered, revealing to the enemy their numbers and weaponry. Then God orchestrates the collapse of Jericho's walls, they destroy the city, and Israel gains its first military victory within Canaan.

Unfortunately, one Israelite, Achan, disobeyed God's plain directive and kept part of the forbidden plunder for himself, leading to a subsequent military defeat by a tiny opposing force and the death of dozens of Israelite soldiers in what otherwise should have been an easy victory. To rectify this wrong, Israel had to stone the offender before successfully continuing the conquest.

Not long after this, Israel's leaders make a grave mistake: When approached by a delegation claiming to have traveled from a distant land, they make a peace treaty with the group *without* first asking the Lord how to proceed. They've been hoodwinked; these men are from a people within Canaan. Now because Israel has sworn an oath not to harm them, not only are they unable to drive them out of the land as God has commanded (Numbers 33:51–52), but they end up facing a whole coalition of armies from south-central Canaan when they defend their new allies.

With God's clear aid, Israel defeats the coalition and sweeps through the now vulnerable region, conquering the major cities. They also defeat a coalition from northern Israel, further opening the highlands of northern and central Canaan for settlement.

The third section of Joshua describes how the twelve tribes divided the land by trusting God to direct the process through the casting of lots. Although the descriptions of areas and lists of cities make for tedious reading today, this section served the critical function of clarifying who was entitled to which land. It also further demonstrated the process of God's fulfilling his ancient promise to give Canaan to Israel. Abraham's many descendants were bound to the Lord in a protective covenant and could now settle in their homeland.

The final section wraps up the era's major events. Joshua gathers the leaders of the now ensconced Israelites and charges them to remain faithful to God, just as he had done. Later he assembles the nation a final time and leads them to recommit themselves to their national covenant with God; their future success in the land will depend on their faithfulness.

Significance

Overall, the book of Joshua records a bright spot in Israel's history. God faithfully fulfills his promises, and, at least for this generation, the people remain largely obedient and enjoy great success. They take much of the land of Canaan, serving as God's instrument of judgment on those who long defied him, refusing to turn from evil and instead hardening in wickedness to the point where God could not permit them to live.

God Faithfully Fulfills His Promises

God had guaranteed Canaan to Abraham's descendants, a pledge he had repeated numerous times to the following generations. The clan lived for a time in Canaan, among its other inhabitants, without seeing the fulfillment of that promise. Then their descendants lived for centuries in Egypt and suffered persecution and slavery while waiting for God to act. Finally, after six or eight centuries (depending on the dating of the events), God delivered Israel, guided them through a literal wilderness, and empowered them to conquer and settle their long-promised home. In these events, God not only shows himself faithful to his people but also reveals both his patience and justice in biding his time to judge Canaan's other peoples.

Israel Succeeds When Obedient

Israel finally received the Promised Land because they obeyed and God was faithful. The generation prior to the conquest died in the desert because they rebelled against God. The next generation obeyed his commands by revealing themselves to the defenders of Jericho before attacking, by believing that the walls of Jericho would collapse at a shout, by executing Achan for taking forbidden plunder, and by trusting they could defeat two coalitions of enemy armies. Because they obeyed, God responded with aid to ensure victory.

Conquest of Canaan—Was This Truly Justice?

Despite the fulfillment of promises and commendable obedience recorded in Joshua, many readers today are troubled by Israel's killing of the Canaanites in order to conquer the land. What's more, the Bible records that God ordered these acts, which to some sound like war crimes, even genocide.

How should a modern reader view such texts? First, to ancient Near Easterners, such actions probably didn't seem extraordinary. The era's literature contains many similar stories regarding one people taking another's land (e.g., cf. Numbers 21:26; Deuteronomy 2:12, 20–23).

Second, and far more significant, the Bible makes clear that God was using the army of Israel to judge the peoples of Canaan for their sins, just as he would later use the armies of Assyria and Babylon to judge the Israelites when they would not turn from their sins. All those centuries during which Abraham's descendants wondered how and when God would fulfill his pledge, were some of the same centuries during which God was patiently enduring the evil of the peoples of Canaan, giving them time, and time, and more time to turn from their wickedness.

God is patient (Genesis 15:16; 2 Peter 3:9) and he is just; he would not have commanded Israel to destroy people unjustly.

For all the differences between how people related to God then and how we relate to him now, God still expects his people to obey him and to wait patiently for him to act. We may want God to act *now*, but the book of Joshua demonstrates how he may choose to wait years, even centuries, to carry out his purposes. We must acknowledge that God is God, and we are not; we must be willing to accept that God will act when and how he knows is best for all parties concerned.

Judges

Setting

Judges records a period of Israelite history that covers approximately three hundred years, from the death of Joshua to the beginning of the monarchy. In contrast to Israel's general obedience, unity, and success during the conquest, this era yields internal strife and flagrant disloyalty to the divine covenant. These help to foster one of the darkest periods of the nation's history, which Israel in turn will survive because their ever-loyal God repeatedly rescues his often faithless people.

During this era God uses twelve military and civil leaders known as judges (perhaps best thought of as deliverers) to free his people from oppressive foreign powers. While these leaders bring relief from external pressures, they often exhibit serious flaws and do not fully lead the nation out of its moral and political quagmire.

Summary

The book of Judges is divided into three sections. The first describes Israel's incomplete conquest of Canaan and the beginning of the nation's descent into apostasy and chaos (1:1–3:6). The Lord had commanded Israel to completely drive out or destroy the inhabitants of the land, but they failed to fully follow his order (e.g., Joshua 13:13; 17:13; Judges 1:32). The second section tells the stories of the judges (3:7–16:31), including both their successes and failures. The third records distasteful stories of moral and spiritual failure that lead to civil war (17:1–21:25)—the final sordid picture of this dark epoch.

The first section begins with God helping the faithful tribe of Judah continue to expel Canaanites (1:1–20). Their obedience contrasts with the failure of the Benjamites (1:21); this, along with the mixed results of the other tribes, leads to God's judgment on the nation. When later Israelites find themselves drawn into the idolatry of the remaining outsiders, God punishes them with oppressors who plunder their crops and other goods. When the Israelites repent and cry out to God for help, he relents and raises up judges to deliver them. That cycle of sin, oppression, outcry, and deliverance repeats itself multiple times during this era.

The book of Judges' second and largest section recounts the exploits of the judges whom God graciously raises up to rescue the oppressed and repentant Israelites. The text describes some with brief accounts (minor judges) and others with longer stories (major judges). Again and again these records demonstrate one of the Old Testament's most prevalent themes: God's faithfulness toward his often unfaithful people. They also highlight the increasingly flawed nature of the deliverers called to aid God's people.

The first major judges meet with success. Othniel, a Judean, inaugurates forty years of peace by defeating an enemy from Mesopotamia. Ehud, a judge from Benjamin, delivers Israel from the Moabites (foes from the southeast) by cunningly slaying their king and so bringing eighty years of relief. Deborah brings four decades of peace by leading Israel to victory over a Canaanite coalition.

Later, Gideon vanquishes the Midianites, a vastly larger foe from the eastern desert, yet follows this by fighting fellow Israelites (from Ephraim) and eventually leads the nation into idolatry. When his son Abimelech succeeds him, he kills all but one of his seventy-one brothers before fighting with and then being slain by his own subjects.

This downward path continues with the last major judges. Jephthah defeats the Ammonites but makes a foolish vow that costs his daughter's life and also ends up killing 42,000 of his own countrymen. The colorful, strong, and brave Samson carries out great exploits but also commits great sins. God had set aside Samson before his birth (13:7; cf. Numbers 6:1–21), yet during his lifetime Samson fails in every facet of this calling. He also consorts with prostitutes and takes a pagan wife.

Judges closes with sordid tales that include theft, idolatry, corrupted worship, rape, and a civil war that nearly wipes out the entire tribe of Benjamin. This account not only casts a dark shadow over the tribe but also echoes earlier accounts demonstrating how depraved Israel has become. The men of Gibeah sin like Sodomites (Genesis 18–19); the other tribes attack Benjamin like Joshua attacked Canaanite Ai (Joshua 8). During the period of the judges, Israel has become like the Canaanites they should have driven out.

Significance

Leadership Matters

On a human plane, Israel had gained its freedom from slavery and secured its land largely because of the effective leadership of Moses and Joshua. Without a strong replacement to assume that mantle, the nation plummets. On the whole, the judges provide a measure of leadership but with inconsistent and limited success. Because they would not simply obey God, Israel needed kings to rule the people.

Failure to Obey Has Consequences

To the extent the Israelites obeyed God's commands, they conquered Canaan. After the conquest, their obedience wanes; by failing to drive out all the local inhabitants as God ordered, they were left in the midst of idolatry and failed to resist its temptations. As a result of failing to gain all the land God had promised, their goods became plunder for outside powers. Just as obedience is rewarded, disobedience proves costly.

God Remains Faithful

Though the Israelites repeatedly break their covenant promise to worship God alone, he delivers them from trouble when they return to him. God doesn't eradicate all the consequences of their sins, but he rescues and restores and blesses them when they repent. God's people often prove unfaithful; he remains ever faithful.

It's as true now as it was then: Effective leadership and obedience are essential to gain God's best, individually and corporately. And sin has destructive effects. Though all of God's people fail at least occasionally, we know that he is faithful and merciful, and when we ask, he will deliver as he knows best.

Ruth

Setting

The story of Ruth takes place during the spiritually dark period of the judges, when seemingly few Israelites fulfilled their covenantal obligations to God or their fellow people. However, this book shows that some did demonstrate such loyalty, including Boaz, a Judean from Bethlehem, and Ruth, a poor widow from Moab.

The book itself does not state who wrote it, but the connection to David at the end and the overall favorable portrayal of the heroine from Moab suggest it may have been written during David's reign to defend his Moabite ancestry. The Bible repeatedly documents long-standing animosity between Israel and Moab: the unsavory story of Moabite origins (Genesis 19:30–38); Moab's king enticing Balaam to curse Israel (Numbers 22–25:5); ongoing clashes through the time of the judges and the monarchy (Judges 3:12–30; 1 Samuel 14:47; 2 Kings 3); and David's brutal conquest of these distant relatives who earlier had aided him (2 Samuel 8:2; 1 Samuel 22:3–4). God said, "No . . . Moabite or any of their descendants may enter the assembly of the LORD, not even in the tenth generation" (Deuteronomy 23:3). This book seems to show that God made an exception for Ruth, and so David was not disqualified from ruling due to this part of his heritage.

Summary

This masterfully written story opens with a brief description of the tragedy that befalls Naomi, a woman from Bethlehem. It then shows how God quietly and graciously resolves her situation through selfless acts of loyalty by others, especially her daughter-in-law Ruth. Largely because of Ruth, the destitute Naomi regains a means of support, a family, and even the honor of a place in the family line of Israel's greatest king (and ultimately of the Messiah). In chapter 1, a famine in Israel prompts Naomi and her husband to move to Moab with their two sons. The sons marry Moabite women, one of whom is Ruth. Then the husband and sons all die. Suddenly Naomi is a widow in a foreign land without anyone to provide for her.

The famine in Israel had ended; Naomi decides to return to her home because the family's land offers some hope of support. She encourages her daughters-in-law to return to their families of origin, for she has no way to provide for them. Orpah, the other daughter-in-law, departs, yet Ruth remains. With fierce loyalty, she pledges her devotion to Naomi and to Naomi's God. The older woman is bitter at God for her losses, but they reach Bethlehem in time for the barley harvest—a potential source of food.

The story takes a significant turn for the better in chapter 2. Ruth dutifully goes into the fields to glean (gather small quantities of grain left by harvesters) in order to obtain food for herself and Naomi. God had commanded Israelite landowners to share from their harvests of grain and other crops by leaving the last bits of the produce for the poor to gather (Deuteronomy 24:19–22). Though he had commanded this, it was likely not all landowners allowed it, especially during this generally disobedient era. However, Ruth "happens" to end up in the field of Boaz, a man of means and also a relative of Ruth's dead father-in-law. Boaz "happens" to meet Ruth, and not only does he allow her to glean in his fields, he goes out of his way to protect and provide extra food for her and Naomi. When Naomi learns of Ruth's success, she is encouraged and begins to consider the possibility of redemption—another God-ordered social custom perhaps not always practiced during this time.

In this form of redemption, a near male relative called a kinsman-redeemer would act to take care of a family member who has fallen into misfortune. For example, if the person had to sell land to pay off debts, the kinsman-redeemer would buy the land back to keep it in the family. If a married man died without male heirs and had no brothers to marry the widow and sire an heir, the kinsman-redeemer would take on this responsibility. Naomi and Ruth needed a relative to redeem them; was there a relative who would?

In chapters 3 and 4, Boaz fulfills this role. First, Naomi encourages Ruth to dress up and meet Boaz at night at the threshing floor, a communal site where farmers processed their harvested grain. Ruth meets Boaz as hoped and asks him to take care of her—meaning, to marry her and purchase the family's land before it is sold to a non-relative. Boaz agrees, but properly follows through by first presenting the opportunity to a man who is a closer relative. That man, in order to preserve his own interests, declines to redeem; by so doing he loses his potential place in the royal lineage. Boaz, by contrast, is selflessly loyal: He buys the land, marries Ruth, and later they have a son whose grandson is King David.

Significance

God Tends to Orchestrate Events Quietly

God directs the events in the book of Ruth in mostly subtle ways, where things seem to work out "coincidentally." Ruth ends up in the fields of Boaz; Boaz comes there at just the right time; the nighttime meeting of Ruth and Boaz at the threshing floor

Ruth

works out perfectly; the closer relative, from self-interest, refuses to redeem the family, so Boaz is able to do so himself. God often provides for his faithful people through (what appears to be) fortunate circumstances and good timing.

God Works to Fix Problems, Often Through His People

God also provides for his people through those who selflessly care for others. The Israelites called this *hesed*—showing loyalty to God and to others as required by their covenant with the Lord. Ruth first showed this loyalty to her mother-in-law, Naomi, and in turn Naomi did likewise to Ruth. Boaz showed his loyalty to God and family by caring for both women.

Though New Testament–era believers aren't bound to the same covenant as were the Old Testament Israelites, God still expects us to demonstrate loyalty to him and to care for others, especially fellow believers. When we do, he orchestrates circumstances so that we are cared for as needed.

1 Samuel

Setting

The book of Samuel—1 Samuel, together with 2 Samuel—describes a period of major transition in the history of Israel. Samuel, the last of Israel's judges, leads a loose federation of largely independent tribes and helps facilitate the difficult transition to centralized governance under a king. He also plays a key role in the book's second major transition—from King Saul (of the tribe of Benjamin) to David (of the tribe of Judah).

The books of 1 and 2 Samuel, originally written as one work, were divided for convenience when translated into Greek before the time of Christ. Samuel—judge, prophet, and high priest—may have written the first part of the book; the author of the rest is unknown. The book describes both the human and divine aspects of many political, military, and theological events during this period that so markedly changed Israel.

Summary

First Samuel traces the career of two rulers, Samuel and Saul—Israel's final judge and its first king. It also introduces a third, David, whose rise creates irreconcilable conflict with the established but ineffective King Saul. The events that transpire between Saul and David reveal who should serve as king and retain the right to pass on the crown to his descendants.

Chapters 1 through 7 follow the career of Samuel, who likewise proves more capable than his own predecessor: Eli, the established but ineffective high priest. Born as God's gift to a formerly barren woman, Samuel demonstrates divine blessing from the start. All Israel can see the contrast between him and Eli's wicked sons. God uses the Philistines to wipe out Eli's line, but when the Philistines defeat Israel, they also capture the ark of the covenant. Although this most holy symbol of the Israelite faith had become a war trophy, God uses the aftermath to show his sovereignty over all other gods. He twice causes the statue of the Philistine god Dagon to fall prostrate before him, and he strikes the Philistines with plagues until they return the ark to Israel.

Chapters 8 through 12 describe Israel's change to monarchy. Samuel leads effectively, but the Israelites see that his sons will not make worthy successors, so they petition him for a king. Earlier Scripture had anticipated a monarchy in Israel, and God knew that the people ultimately would demand a king (Genesis 17:16; 49:10; Numbers 24:17–19; Deuteronomy 17:14–20). Yet the request still displeases both him and Samuel, who warns the Israelites of the pitfalls of kingly rule. When the people don't relent, God chooses Saul, and Samuel anoints him privately. While God confirms Saul's selection through miraculous signs and a public ceremony, Saul shies away from the moment and fails to obey all of Samuel's instructions—a sad harbinger of things to come.

Saul's subsequent reign highlights his failure to obey God and to serve as king. He begins well, rescuing an Israelite city from grave military danger, but this proves a singular event. Fearing a superior foe, Saul disobeys an explicit order from Samuel and, by choosing his own way over following God, he forfeits the chance to begin a dynasty. He then makes a foolish vow and nearly kills his own son, Jonathan, to fulfill it. Finally, he disobeys another requirement from God and loses even his own right to rule.

Chapters 16 through 31 witness David's star rising to eclipse Saul's. As he'd done with Saul, Samuel anoints the young man who will become Israel's second king, though David won't begin to reign immediately. He does serve the crown, first as a court musician and then as a warrior; he defeats Goliath and rescues Israel from another Philistine threat. Saul's murderous envy causes David first to flee his court and then the entire kingdom in fear for his life. Twice during this time, David refuses to kill Saul, even in self-defense, choosing instead to wait on God's timing. As he'd done with Eli and Samuel, God uses the Philistines to remove Saul's line so that David can take over. During the years of running from Saul, David shows his leadership ability by building a loyal private army. He also exhibits political savvy and strong moral character by refusing to kill the duly established (though largely unfit) ruler. These traits serve him well when later he raises Israel to glory as its greatest and most famous king.

Significance

God Uses People of Great Character, Regardless of Their Background

God substitutes Samuel for Eli and David for Saul. Neither Samuel nor David is in the "right" family (according to tribe) to replace the established leaders, but God elevates each of them nonetheless. God establishes the lines of priests and kings for Israel, yet makes exceptions for people of surpassing character.

God Deals With People in Light of Their Choices

God directs the events in Israel in part because of people's choices. Hannah asks for a son; Samuel is a blessing both to her and to the nation. The Israelites refuse to reconsider their clamoring for a king; they suffer under the king's ineffective leadership. Saul makes a series of wrong decisions; he loses God's blessing, the opportunity to begin a dynasty, the right to his own kingship, and finally the lives of his sons as well as his own. By contrast, David makes wise choices; he earns God's favor, the kingship, and an enduring dynasty that extends infinitely through the eternal reign of Jesus.

God Takes Time to Make Things Right

God placed Samuel and David into their places of service, but from a human perspective he took a long time to do it. Under Eli and Saul the nation longed for more effective leadership. David long suffered Saul's mistreatment, waiting for what God had promised—for what he'd already been anointed to do! Those who trusted and obeyed God were put into the right spots, and they didn't have to force their way or their own timetable.

Most believers today don't live in Israel or under the rule of kings, but God still directs events in our world and in our lives as he sees fit. He likewise still uses people of strong character and blesses those who make wise choices. God's plans and purposes are never frustrated and always come to fruition, whether or not they happen when we want them to or how we think they should.

2 Samuel

Setting

The book of Samuel was originally a single composition; 2 Samuel continues where 1 Samuel leaves off.

Saul has just died in battle, leaving Israel with diminished confidence that it can survive its internal conflicts or the continuing threats from the Philistines and other neighboring peoples. The nation's best hope lies with David, a gifted former shepherd from Bethlehem. Years before, the prophet Samuel had anointed him, and now the path to the crown is open. David moves skillfully not only to assume the throne but also to raise Israel to regional dominance. In the process, God rewards him with a covenant that promises unending dynastic succession. Unfortunately, David's personal failings also create tremendous turmoil within his family and his kingdom.

For a brief discussion of the history and authorship of 1 and 2 Samuel, see "Setting" of 1 Samuel.

Summary

Chapters 1 through 4 present Israel attempting to recover from devastating defeat. Philistia, a clearly superior enemy, has just killed Saul, the king, and Jonathan, the crown prince, while decimating the army. The northern tribes* crown another of Saul's sons, Ish-Bosheth, to rule in his place. David, Saul's formal rival, also is crowned by his own tribe, Judah, in far southern Israel. Several years of strife ensue and further fracture the divided nation. Support for David gradually increases, and he eventually becomes king over the entire nation, deftly avoiding complicity in the deaths of his remaining rivals. Israel emerges from the crisis unified under a capable, ambitious king poised to lead the nation to greatness.

Chapters 5 through 12 describe how David consolidates and expands Israel's strength until it becomes the region's strongest power. First, he moves its capital from Hebron to Jerusalem, a more central location that allows for adequate defense as well as expansion. He then inflicts decisive defeat on the Philistines, a nemesis since the time of Samson.

Somewhat surprisingly, David's subsequent attempts to make Jerusalem into Israel's religious center sputter; he encounters problems bringing the ark of the covenant to the city, and God postpones for a generation David's plan to build a permanent temple there. God does honor David's character and service by promising him a line of perpetual royal succession, an honor denied to Saul (see Psalm 89; 132).

David's sin with Bathsheba interrupts this account of his considerable triumphs. God has given David a crown, riches, immense honor, and military renown, but he does not grant the king pardon to conquer another man's wife. Although David earnestly repents of his adultery and God forgives him, his moral failure causes

---

*Reuben, Benjamin, Issachar, Zebulun, Dan, Naphtali, Gad, Asher, Ephraim, and Manasseh. Later these ten tribes together will become known as the northern kingdom.

tremendous conflict within his family and in the kingdom for the rest of his reign.

The balance of the book records the sad decline for the king, his family, and his kingdom. David's son Amnon rapes and then abandons his half-sister, Tamar. Tamar's brother Absalom kills Amnon in revenge and as a result spends several years in exile. After Absalom returns, David spurns him; Absalom eventually rebels, seeking both to seize the crown and end his father's life. Though David overcomes the challenge, he mishandles the achievement by mourning and honoring his seditious son instead of praising and showing gratitude to those who faithfully stood by him. In sharp contrast to his political skill, military acumen, and spiritual vitality, David struggled mightily to govern his family well.

Significance

Actions Yield Corresponding Results

At the beginning of 2 Samuel, Israel is in desperate straits partly because of the poor choices of its prior king. Even so, Israel rises to prominence largely because of the wise choices of its next ruler. King David does not always choose as wisely as the shepherd David had; in consequence, he, his family, and his nation suffer profoundly. Human choices yield corresponding fruit, for good or for bad, both personally and corporately.

How We Respond to Failure Matters Greatly

Both Saul and David commit grave sins, but unlike Saul, David responds well after his failure. When confronted about his sin with Bathsheba, David confesses and turns back to God (cf. Psalm 51). The Lord responds with forgiveness, and while he does not spare David or his people all the consequences of what he's done, neither does he take away his crown or the honor of dynastic succession.

God Uses the Line of David to Bless His People

God blesses David with an eternal covenant (known as the Davidic covenant; 7:1–27) through which he uses David's royal descendants to bless his people despite their failures. David kept his throne despite his mistakes; his descendants ruled in Jerusalem nearly four hundred years after him, even though they sinned. David's greatest descendant, Jesus, now rules in heaven and will one day rule on earth—blessing us despite our failures.

Christians must bear in mind that we will benefit or suffer from our decisions and actions. Even if we're wise enough to choose well most of the time, we all sometimes fail. We should likewise consider that how we respond to failure plays a key role in how God will direct our course in life.

1 Kings

Setting (1 and 2 Kings)

The books of 1 and 2 Kings conclude the account of the people of Israel living in the Promised Land before the time of their exile. This story began back in Genesis, when God started a line of people with Abraham and pledged to give them the land of Canaan as their home. Abraham's descendants eventually did conquer that land under Joshua, reached their pinnacle of power and glory under David and Solomon, and remained there for several hundred years until they were conquered and exiled at the hands of Assyria and Babylon.

First and Second Kings begin with the reign of Solomon, continue with the nation's division into Israel and Judah, and follow the rule of their kings over the next four centuries, until finally the two nations are conquered and exiled. They emphasize how the nation and its kings do or do not follow God, particularly in three areas: the loyalty of the kings to their God, the people's worship of God, and the nation's response to the prophets (e.g., Elijah and Elisha) God raises up to call the Israelites to fulfill their covenantal obligations. When his people refuse again and again to heed the warnings, God uses their enemies to conquer them and take them from their land, just as he had warned them long ago through Moses. Like 1 and 2 Samuel, 1 and 2 Kings were originally a single book, but were divided for convenience before the time of Christ. The unknown author(s) of Kings probably wrote this history during the Babylonian exile to explain to the exiled people why this national tragedy occurred: not because God failed his people, but because they failed him.

Summary

The book starts with and dedicates half its total space (1–11) to the reign of Solomon, arguably the zenith of Israel's glory. Though Solomon was David's chosen successor, he first must survive a play for the throne by Adonijah, his half brother. After securing the kingship, Solomon asks God for wisdom to rule well, which God grants. It then describes his phenomenal wisdom, immense wealth, and achievement in erecting Israel's national shrine, the temple. It also implicitly criticizes him for amassing military power, wealth, and numerous wives, all in violation of God's clear prohibition (Deuteronomy 17:16–17). Those many wives lead Solomon into idolatry, which causes God to tear away much of the kingdom from the Davidic dynasty.

Chapters 12 through 14 describe the division of Israel into two kingdoms, with Judah in the south following the line of David, and the larger, more powerful Israel in the north following a separate line of kings. God gives the northern crown first to Jeroboam, a former official of Solomon, because of his loyalty to God. But then Jeroboam establishes a rival religious system in the north, violating God's command to worship only in Jerusalem (see Deuteronomy 12). All northern kings thereafter would support this heretical system and thus they "did evil in the eyes of the LORD" (1 Kings 15:26ff.).

Chapters 15 through 22 alternately note the reigns of the northern and southern kings, briefly emphasizing each ruler's loyalty or disloyalty to God and noting any particular achievements or other significant events that occurred during his reign. The rule of one northern king, Ahab, marks a critical juncture. Influenced by his Phoenician wife, Jezebel, Ahab pushes Israel to worship the Canaanite god Baal; God raises up the prophet Elijah to challenge the nation to remain loyal to him. With the Lord's power, Elijah wins the dramatic encounter with Baal's prophets on Mount Carmel, yet still he cannot steer Israel from its destructive path toward apostasy and exile.

Significance

God Expects His People to Obey His Commands

God had made clear that he expected his people to worship only him and only as prescribed. He also told them to heed the warnings of his prophets. Both the kings and the people ultimately failed in each of these areas. Though for centuries he would patiently hold back judgment (conquest by foreign powers and exile from the land), consequences would surely follow, for they would not change their ways.

Leaders Are Even More Responsible for Their Actions

The spiritual loyalty and effective leadership of David, and for a time Solomon, bring the nation the honor and security God intends for his people. But the subsequent disloyalty of kings and people lead to division and weakness, and eventually result in expulsion from their beloved homeland. All God's people bear responsibility to follow his commands under their national covenant with him.

However, as God's anointed leaders, the kings are most responsible. Through Moses, God spelled out specific directives for future rulers (Deuteronomy 17:16–17) long before Israel's first king, and no king is excused or exempt from following what the Lord has prescribed.

Today we don't have specific national covenants with God, yet his general rules of conduct still apply (e.g., Proverbs 14:34). Whether or not he waits many years to visit upon us the consequences of our wrong actions, his justice is certain. If we disobey him, negative results will surely follow.

2 Kings

Setting

See "Setting (1 and 2 Kings)" under 1 Kings.

Summary

Second Kings carries on the tragic story of what had become of the kingdoms of Israel and Judah—the nation founded by God and the dynasty of kings to whom he had promised perpetual rule. That nation, blessed like no other, nonetheless had already suffered division; now it would undergo further decline, and eventually conquest and exile. Second Kings concludes the history up to the exile (of the northern kingdom by Assyria, of the southern kingdom by Babylon) and explains why it met such an inglorious end.

Chapters 1 through 8 describe the ministries of the prophets Elijah and Elisha. They sought to turn the nation back from worshiping the Canaanite god Baal and restore faithful worship of the Lord. These stories continue to emphasize the prophets' miraculous power and the certainty of their predictive messages.

Chapters 9 through 17 give the dual history of the northern and southern kingdoms (Israel and Judah) up until Israel is conquered by the powerful kingdom of Assyria. The author emphasizes the general lack of religious purity of the kings, especially in the north, whose kings continue the heretical system Jeroboam had set up. Later, Ahab moves his kingdom toward outright worship of Baal. In response, God uses Jehu, a military general, to usurp the throne and annihilate Ahab's line. The southern kings show varying levels of fidelity in worship—for example, Josiah renovates God's temple, but Manasseh sacrifices his own son to a pagan god.

The two kingdoms during this period experience frequent turmoil from both internal and external causes. The north endures frequent coups with resulting changes in dynastic lines. While the south enjoys the stability of rule by the Davidic line, at one point Athaliah, the queen mother, nearly wipes out the rest of her family in order to take the throne. Further, the Aramean kingdom to the north is often at war with Israel and sometimes Judah. Then, in the eighth century BC, the more distant Mesopotamian kingdoms of Assyria and Babylon begin to impact and later dominate affairs in both Israel and Judah. In 721 BC the northern kingdom, Israel, falls to Assyria, and much of its population is deported.

Chapters 18 through 25 recount the last century and a half of Judah's history after Israel had fallen. While the southern kingdom is blessed by the reigns of Hezekiah and Josiah, two godly kings who follow the Lord's commands, sadly they are the exceptions. Most Judean kings are chronically unfaithful—some even erect altars to foreign gods in Yahweh's temple. In the end, God uses Babylon to conquer Judah and destroy Jerusalem and the temple in 586 BC. Even so, God is not finished with his people. Just as the prophets had predicted this exile, they also foretold restoration afterward. The faithful God who fulfilled his promise to punish disobedience would faithfully restore those who had been brought low.

Significance

Why Israel and Judah Suffered Conquest and Exile

The author of 2 Kings wrote to explain clearly why the nation suffered conquest and exile: "All this took place because the Israelites had sinned against the LORD. . . . They worshiped other gods. . . . The LORD warned Israel and Judah through all his prophets. . . . But they would not listen. . . . So the LORD . . . removed them from his presence" (17:7–18).

Israel's Kings Failed, Yet Promise Hope

The kings of Israel and Judah largely do not live up to their calling, and these failures are a major cause of the exile. Nevertheless, 2 Kings concludes with Jehoiachin, one of Judah's final kings, gaining freedom from prison in exile, projecting hope for the future of God's people and even of the Davidic line. The people's sins don't end God's gracious plans for them. God will restore them to their land, and one of David's descendants will rule forever. Part of Israel's future includes God raising up a truly righteous "Son of David" (Jesus), whose perfect reign will never end.

The hope 2 Kings portrays for the Davidic line and for God's people is a promise that will culminate in Jesus, the King of Kings. In his first coming, Jesus suffers to cover our sin. When he returns, he will set up his glorious eternal reign (Revelation 20–22). Never ending Davidic rule will be fully realized. God's people will be fully blessed.

1 Chronicles

Setting (1 and 2 Chronicles)

At first glance, 1 and 2 Chronicles seem primarily to repeat much of the information from 1 and 2 Kings, and only the long genealogical section at the beginning of 1 Chronicles stands out as new. If both the repetition and the long genealogy cause challenges for many readers today, such would not have been the case for the original audience.

These books were written by an unknown author to those who had recently returned from Babylonian exile in great need of hope. The earlier 1 and 2 Kings had explained to the people *during* the exile that they suffered conquest and expulsion because of their sin and failure to keep their covenant with God. Now those back in their land *after* the exile needed encouragement for what lay ahead. They'd survived, but they'd come back to a smaller, poorer, badly struggling Judah. They needed to know and remember that God's promises about David and the temple offered hope for a brighter future, including a coming leader (the Messiah).

As with the books of Samuel and Kings, Chronicles initially was written as a single book, and before the time of Christ was divided for the sake of convenience.

Summary

Although 1 and 2 Chronicles do retell the history of Israel, there are several important differences. For example, Chronicles uses genealogy to link its readers to the past, thereby helping the returnees from exile reestablish much of the fabric of their society. Also, Chronicles focuses on Judah and the Davidic dynasty, and largely on the positive aspects of past kings, especially David and Solomon.

The long genealogy that opens 1 Chronicles (1–9) connects surviving Judahites—or Jews—all the way back to Adam. This helped anchor them historically, and it described the tribal lines within their nation. Much of the culture was based on family connections, such as rights to property and position, and military and other obligations. When the kingdom was overthrown and most of the people were banished from the land, a large part of the population had been wiped out, records were lost, and the nation's infrastructure was severely damaged. How could they rebuild and move ahead? In part, by reestablishing themselves along family lines.

The other major part of 1 Chronicles (10–29) begins this history with a long section on David that omits most of the negative stories recorded in Kings and highlights instead his successes— especially his preparations for building the temple. Early events like the transition of rule from Saul to David and David's conquest of Jerusalem serve mainly to set the stage for planning of the temple. When God did not allow David himself to build it, David made extensive preparations, including plans, materials, and organization, and passed these on to his son Solomon along with the charge to complete the project. First Chronicles ends with Israel's greatest two kings working in concert to establish the place where the nation would worship its God.

Significance

The First Temple Can Encourage the Building of Its Replacement

The author stresses the best aspects of the best kings to highlight two developments that will help later Jews in the days to come. First, he emphasizes what had been the preparations for the first temple in order to encourage the returnees from exile to build the second one. Centuries before, Israel's greatest leaders had built a grand temple at the peak of the kingdom's national glory. It had been destroyed and God was now commanding the Israelites to rebuild it (see also under "Ezra"). The account of the original temple was to inspire them to fulfill this charge; even if the nation was now much poorer than it had been, God would see the project through successfully.

In Blessing God's People, David and Solomon Prefigure the Messiah

Chapter 17 records God's promise to David that he would have an eternal line of succession. Israel's sin and resulting exile interrupted this rule and its blessing for Israel, but they did not cancel the promise. God would restore David's line, and a future anointed descendant would bless Israel as David and Solomon had, and far more so. As the author implies, the Messiah would exhibit their best qualities.

God used 1 Chronicles to give its original readers hope for the future. He reminded them of what he'd done in the past: specifically establishing them as a people and blessing them so that they could build the temple. Believers today who look back at what God has done for them likewise should be encouraged and strengthened in their faith that he will guide and bless their future as well.

2 Chronicles

Setting

See "Setting (1 and 2 Chronicles)" under 1 Chronicles.

Summary

The second part of Chronicles continues the focus on David and Solomon in order to encourage its readers. Its longest section (1–9) describes Solomon's reign, highlighting his wisdom and riches and his construction of the nation's first temple. Thus, more than half of 1 and 2 Chronicles is dedicated to these two kings, with the goal of inspiring the struggling audience of the time with reminders of their nation's past greatness. God would restore rule to the Davidic line. The people, their hope placed in God, could bank on a coming messianic ruler who would restore Israel's glory.

A brief section that follows (10–12) highlights events from the reign of Solomon's son Rehoboam, including foolish decisions that helped precipitate Israel's division and his own failure to follow God's law faithfully. However, it also notes his humility when prophetically rebuked, which resulted in God's mercy.

Rehoboam's rule formed something of a pattern for the rest of the southern rulers (13–36). When they failed to obey God, especially by turning to idolatry, he punished them. When they obeyed, particularly in leading the nation to worship God aright, he blessed them. Sadly, the former was far more common than the latter, culminating in the Babylonian conquest and exile.

Significance

Sin Has Consequences

The book's historical recap clearly illustrates sin's effects, both for individual kings and for the nation as a whole. Kings who err suffer in their lifetimes. Accumulated effects of the nation's sins play out over its history: losses of glory, wealth, health, freedom, and blessing, and sometimes life itself.

God Is Always Willing to Forgive and Restore

But just as certainly as God visits the costs of faithless actions on the kings and the people, so he forgives them when they repent. Kings who humble themselves and repent receive his mercy, as do nations: God forgives them of their sins and then restores them to their land. By the time Chronicles is written, God promises not only that he will help the Jews survive the hardships they're enduring, but he will also bring them greater blessing in the future.

Believers today don't relate to God through the Mosaic covenant as did Israel. But just as sin still has consequences, so God is still ready to forgive and restore when we humble ourselves and repent.

Ezra

Setting

The book of Ezra describes events that occur from the latter part of the sixth century to the latter part of the fifth century BC, a time of major upheaval in the ancient Near East. Cyrus the Great of Persia had conquered Babylon (in 539 BC) and annexed to his empire the many lands and peoples the Babylonians had previously conquered. Cyrus decreed that all exiled peoples, including the Jews, could now return to their own homelands. Ezra opens with this decree and continues as the exiled Jews return to their land and seek to restore their homes, their lives, and especially their worship of God.

The first part of the book is written as a history of the Jewish return from exile (sixth century). The second part is comprised of personal memoirs from Ezra, the priest and scribe who describes his activities (fifth century) as he works to restore the Jewish people. He may have written the earlier part also, or perhaps someone else compiled the book during or shortly after his time (c. 430 BC) near the end of Old Testament history.

Summary

Chapters 1 through 6 tell how a group of Jews returns from captivity and rebuilds their temple despite numerous difficulties. Cyrus's decree (539 BC), which allows their return, fulfills Jewish prophecy (Isaiah 44:28; Jeremiah 29:10).

In 538 BC, fifty thousand Jews make the long journey back to Judea and immediately start work to restore worship at the temple's ruins. Led by their Jewish governor, Zerubbabel, and Joshua, a priest, they rebuild the altar of sacrifice in the temple courtyard and begin sacrifices as prescribed by Mosaic law. They also lay the new temple's foundation.

Strong opposition quickly arises from nearby peoples. During the exile, leaders of these neighboring groups had enjoyed positions of power in the region; a resurgent Jewish presence threatens that status quo. The opponents persuade the Persian king to stop the Jews from finishing the temple.

The Jews eventually regain permission from King Darius, and by 516 BC they complete the work. The returned exiles celebrate the temple's dedication, since it signifies God's presence among them as well as their renewed allegiance to him.

In chapters 7 through 10 (458–c. 433 BC), Ezra describes how he led a smaller, later group of returning Jews and recounts his subsequent efforts to reform Jewish religious and social practice. Before Ezra departs for Judah, King Artaxerxes commissions him to return and help revive Jewish worship, supplying him with money in support of those efforts. After Ezra and his group complete the four-month trip, they use the Persian funds to purchase animals for sacrifice as well as other necessities.

Ezra finds he must confront a major problem that has cropped up—Jews have been intermarrying with local people who serve idols. Just as earlier Israelites needed to avoid mixing with the Canaanites, so the returnees must now turn from similar temptation. If they don't, their children will be drawn to idolatry and reject

God, which led to the exile in the first place. The book ends as Ezra leads the people in confessing this sin; the matter is so serious that he challenges the guilty to divorce their pagan wives.

Significance

God Faithfully Fulfills His Promises

God had fulfilled his warning that he would exile the people if they broke faith with him (Deuteronomy 28:36); now he fulfills his promise to bring them back. King Cyrus may think he allows the exiles to return in order to promote widespread loyalty to his empire through kinder policies, but he also does it "in order to fulfill the word of the LORD" (Ezra 1:1; cf. Isaiah 44:28; Jeremiah 29:10).

God's People Are to Show Their Faithfulness to Him

After God fulfills these promises to his people, they need to respond in appropriate faithfulness to what he has asked of them. In this case they need to rebuild the temple despite opposition, lack of resources, and competing priorities, while they likewise endeavor to rebuild their society. They especially must remain faithful to God's command to avoid intermarrying with the idolatrous peoples around them.

No matter how different our situation and circumstances today, God is ever faithful to us, and we need to be faithful to him. He doesn't call us to contribute financially to a temple in Jerusalem, but he may call us to give sacrificially to other parts of his ongoing work—perhaps through our church or other ministries. And while we may not be tempted to wed Canaanite pagans, we must resist enticements from corrupting influences.

Nehemiah

Setting

The book of Nehemiah records how God continues to restore his people back into their homeland after captivity in Babylon, largely through governor Nehemiah's effective leadership. The book is named for its principal character, a Jew born in exile who serves major roles in Persia's government. King Artaxerxes authorizes Nehemiah to return as governor to help restore Judah, a vassal state in the vast Persian Empire. The book chronicles Nehemiah's struggles and successes in fulfilling his royally (and divinely) commissioned task.

Much like the book of Ezra, Nehemiah describes events c. 445–432 BC (see also "Setting" under Ezra). Like Ezra, the book of Nehemiah includes personal memoirs as well as various lists and other historical material. The original compiler, possibly Ezra, apparently produced Ezra and Nehemiah as a single work, for the earliest manuscripts treat them as a unit; only later, when translated, were they separated. The two books describe how faithful Jews work under God's protection and blessing to help restore his covenantal people.

Summary

Chapters 1 through 6 describe the efforts and challenges Nehemiah faced in physically restoring Jerusalem, the capital of his ancestral homeland. The book begins with him serving the Persian king as cupbearer, a position of great responsibility and trust. Nehemiah, hearing that the Jews who'd returned to Jerusalem have not managed to rebuild the city's walls, is spurred into action. He gains the king's approval to return as governor of the Persian province that includes Judea, and he makes the journey back to the badly damaged city. He conducts a private, nocturnal survey to determine what is needed to rebuild the walls—essential to protect an ancient city's inhabitants—and enable it to flourish once again.

Nehemiah then gathers the people, exhorts them to join him in rebuilding the walls, and faces subsequent opposition from within and without. External resistance comes from neighboring officials who've enjoyed positions of might in the local administration; they don't want a resurgent Jewish presence that might lessen their power. They physically threaten the builders and deride their efforts: "Can they bring the stones back to life from those heaps of rubble—burned as they are? . . . What they are building—even a fox climbing up on it would break down their wall of stones!" (4:2–3). In addition, internal issues arise when wealthy Jews are wrongly profiting from poor Jews. Nehemiah overcomes all these obstacles with effective defense against those without and economic reform to address injustice within; Jerusalem's wall is completed in less than two months.

Chapters 7 through 13 describe Nehemiah's efforts thereafter to rebuild Jewish society alongside his colleague Ezra. He leads a movement to settle more people in Jerusalem and its surrounding villages. Ezra the priest reads and teaches from the Bible and leads the people to renew their national covenant with God. Nehemiah travels back to Persia temporarily, and finds upon his return to Judea that he must address the people's continuing moral and spiritual struggles. These include not honoring the Sabbath, marrying foreigners (who would not honor the covenant with God), and neglecting tithes and offerings. The book ends with Nehemiah frustrated about these problems, illustrating the ongoing challenges he faces in spurring on God's people to continued faithfulness.

Significance

Effective Leaders Accomplish Tasks for God

When Nehemiah learns about needs back in Judea, he understands what must be done and works effectively and persistently to carry it out. He gets needed governmental approval, gathers information and resources, plans appropriately, assembles his people and motivates them to join in the work, addresses troubles as they arise, and successfully accomplishes his God-given task. This work meaningfully advances God's purposes for his people in Nehemiah's time and place, as other effective leaders do in their worlds.

Opposition Comes Both From Inside and Outside

Nehemiah works on the right task in the right way, yet he still faces challenges—both from inside and outside his community. All believers in leadership positions should expect opposition from those who don't grasp or may oppose God's purposes. Leaders also shouldn't be surprised by problems with or even direct resistance from fellow believers. Self-interest, difference in perspective, and the general turmoil created by corrupted human nature all can produce discord among believers.

When we serve as leaders seeking to help accomplish God's purposes, we need a clear picture of what God calls us to do, and we need to work skillfully and diligently to follow it through. When we're a part of a group of God's people, regardless of any position we may fill, we need to strive to assist the group toward achieving its goals rather than creating obstacles to mutual success.

Esther

Setting

The book of Esther records how God preserves the Jewish people from a grave danger that threatens their very existence in the fifth century BC. A Jewish girl becomes queen of the Persian Empire, courageously helps rescue her people from a dire threat, and inaugurates the Jewish feast of Purim.

The book of Esther is set during the reign of Ahasuerus (his Greek name was Xerxes), who ruled Persia at the peak of its power (485–465 BC). The author is unknown, though his familiarity with Jewish and Persian customs suggests he may have been a Jew who lived in Susa, the Persian capital, and wrote c. 460 BC, not long after the events described. The Jews in this story remained in exile after the Zerubbabel-led group had returned to Judah in 538 BC (cf. Ezra 1–2) and before the returns led by Ezra and Nehemiah (c. 440 BC). The book tells the tale of a beautiful and courageous heroine who rescues her people from a cruel villain, including dramatic reversals that enable good to triumph over evil.

Summary

Chapters 1 through 5 introduce the major characters, show how Esther rose to her surprising place of power, and set up the threat to the Jews by a descendant of one of their ancient enemies. As the book opens, the king is giving a lavish banquet, perhaps just before his ill-fated invasion of Greece in 480 BC. During what should have been a show of his power, the queen, Vashti, challenges the king's authority by refusing to appear as summoned. So Ahasuerus deposes her and the search for a potential replacement puts Esther, the Jewess, in the royal palace. She wins the king's favor and is named queen of Persia, with Ahasuerus unaware of her ethnic heritage. Esther's kinsman, Mordecai, works at the gate to the royal compound, a placement that enables him to overhear and then foil a plot to assassinate the king.

The author notes that Mordecai is from the Israelite tribe of Benjamin and, further, descends from Kish and Shimei (2:5), clearly linking him to Saul, Israel's first king (1 Samuel 9:1; 2 Samuel 16:5). This connection contrasts with the Jews' nemesis, Haman, an Agagite, apparently descended from Agag, an adversary of Saul and of Israel (1 Samuel 15). This ancient animosity plays out again in Esther's day through Haman's hatred for Mordecai. Through his status as royal advisor, Haman successfully manipulates the king's trust and plots to exterminate not only Mordecai, but all the Jews in the empire. In response, Mordecai enlists the aid of his cousin, the queen, whose ability to help could be limited by her lack of access to the king.

The action continues and the threat is resolved in chapters 6 through 10. A series of apparent coincidences, along with fortuitous timing, combine to create several reversals that end with Mordecai in the position that formerly belonged to his enemy and the Jews surviving the threat.

One night Ahasuerus cannot sleep, and so he has a scribe read to him from the royal annals. Upon discovering that Mordecai had not been rewarded for earlier saving his life, the king determines to honor Esther's cousin. Haman arrives at that moment, thinking to procure the king's permission to kill Mordecai; instead, Ahasuerus orders Haman to honor Mordecai. Though humiliated by what he must do, Haman consoles himself with the honor of his invitation to a banquet prepared by the queen for only the king and himself. However, at a second banquet, Esther exposes her racial background and the danger to the lives of her and her people. Furious at being duped, Ahasuerus also witnesses what he interprets as Haman's physical attack on Esther, and he orders Haman's immediate death.

The king then grants to Mordecai the property and position of his former foe, yet because Ahasuerus had signed Haman's decree, the threat to the Jews remains. Such a Persian edict cannot be cancelled; Mordecai issues a second royal decree allowing the Jews to defend themselves on the day of the planned attack against them. Many people die, yet the Jewish people survive the threat. Esther proclaims a perpetual remembrance of this deliverance—the feast of Purim, named for the Persian word *pur* (plural *purim*), for the *lots* Haman had cast to destroy them.

Significance

God Allows Bad Events but Uses Them for Good

This book records many bad events that befall the Jews: the exile, subservience to pagan kingdoms, Esther taken to a king's harem, and the murderous threat posed by an evil official. Yet God makes events work out for the eventual good of his people. Not all survive, some don't survive unscathed, but in the end, God's good purposes prevail.

God Sovereignly but Quietly Guides Events as He Sees Best

While God's sovereign hand is evident in the events of Esther, the author does not overtly point it out. In fact, the book nowhere mentions God, prayer, worship, sacrifice, or the Mosaic covenant. Because of these omissions, some have questioned if Esther even belongs in the Bible. The author seems to highlight God's activity by showing that he is working without actually stating it.

God Preserves His People From Endless Attacks

Just as Haman's attack against Mordecai and the Jews echoed earlier animosity between Saul and Agag, so Jews throughout history have learned that they are the targets of ongoing hatred. Had Haman's plan succeeded, they would have been exterminated, ending God's work through them, including the Messiah to come. Satan continues his war against God's purposes, including attempts to wipe out the people of the covenant.

God worked to help his people and bring about his purposes in this story. No less does he guide events today, sometimes dramatically, but more often subtly, causing history to unfold in such a way as to accomplish his ultimate designs. God's people should take comfort and live with confidence that the King of the universe is in charge.

Job

Setting

Job, one of the Bible's most theologically rich books, addresses why people sometimes suffer in ways they don't deserve, how people should respond to suffering, and where to get the wisdom to manage life's tests and trials. The discussions of these subjects are woven into the fabric of an ancient, poetic, theological dispute that many readers today find difficult to unravel.

Even the setting presents challenges. Job worships the one true God, but apparently he was not an Israelite. He lives in Uz (1:1), the southern Transjordanian region later known as Edom. The events seem to have taken place around Abraham's time (c. 2000 BC), for like many patriarchs, Job lived well past age 140; he acted as priest by offering sacrifices for his family (forbidden after the giving of the Mosaic law); and his wealth was measured in animals. Some have speculated the unknown author may have been Moses; whoever recorded it seems knowledgeable in areas as diverse as astronomy, mining, and nature. He addresses some of life's most perplexing subjects and helps his readers explore both the limits of what humans can know and how we should handle our most vexing dilemmas.

Summary

The book begins and ends with brief sections of simple prose that frame its large poetic heart. The introduction (chapters 1–2) first describes Job as eminently upright and wealthy, clearly blessed by God. It continues with a surprising conversation between God and Satan (the Accuser), in which God points to Job as righteous, and Satan argues that he is good only because of all God gives him. When God grants Satan permission to take Job's wealth and even his children, Job responds with faith and trust: "The LORD gave and the LORD has taken away; may the name of the LORD be praised" (1:21). Defeated but undaunted, Satan receives further permission to rob Job of his health, yet Job responds piously: "Shall we accept good from God, and not trouble?" (2:10). Three men come to comfort their suffering friend by mourning, then sitting with him for seven days in silence.

The attitudes behind the exemplary responses of Job and his friends break down in the book's second section (chapters 3–31). Job breaks the silence to lament his pain and to mourn that he'd ever been born. His friends respond with well-intentioned but ultimately incorrect counsel. They assume his situation must fit the pattern in which obedience to God's commands leads to blessing and disobedience results in suffering. Job is suffering; he must have sinned. From their perspective, Job must repent.

Seemingly unaware of the cosmic interchange between God and Satan in which he plays a key role, Job protests correctly that he is innocent of any wrong that would have caused his suffering. He and his friends engage in increasingly contentious debate about the source of his suffering and the needed resolution. The section ends with both sides convinced they're right but unable to prove the other wrong, and Job longs for the chance to confront God face-to-face and charge him with allowing his unjust suffering.

The book moves close to resolution with the words of a fourth friend (chapters 32–37). Elihu, who has kept silent to this point, rebukes the others for being unable to prove Job's guilt, but also rebukes Job for charging God with wrongdoing: "Far be it from God to do evil" (34:10). Elihu correctly shifts the dispute's focus from Job's situation to the need to look to God as the final source of wisdom, yet his speeches do not resolve the matter. Each of the five understands part of the situation; none is sufficiently wise to solve Job's quandary.

God finally resolves the matter by speaking to Job from a strong wind (38:1–42:6). He does not answer Job's questions and does not even enlighten him about the cause of his suffering. Instead, God challenges Job with question after question, highlighting Job's inability to create, control, or even explain the world God has made. Fully chastised for thinking himself above God in any way, Job repents and submits to the sovereign, all-knowing God. Though he does not get his questions answered, Job comes to recognize the limits of his wisdom. He accepts that only God can grasp his situation fully and that a finite human should trust that the supremely wise Sovereign knows and does what is best.

Significance

People May Suffer in Ways They Don't Deserve or Understand

Readers of the book know from the outset why Job is suffering: *because* he is good and a part of God's greater purpose. Job apparently does not learn this, but he accepts that he does not need to know. He learns to trust that God knows what he does not and always does what is best.

Behavior Does Not ALWAYS Correlate With Results

The Bible shows that right behavior is rewarded and bad behavior brings pain—most of the time. However, the Bible also includes a number of exceptions to that rule, like Job. The general rule has exceptions; Job's friends erred in not allowing for this.

How Should God's People Respond to Suffering?

Job can't understand the reason for his suffering, so he asks, *"Why?"* God does not rebuke Job for asking, but is displeased when Job's frustration rises to demand answers from God. The creature must never place himself above the Creator, nor should a limited human ever think he knows everything. Each person in the story understood part of the situation, but none understood enough to bring about resolution. They needed to trust in the all-knowing God who did know the whole picture and could resolve the matter.

Like Job, people today sometimes suffer in ways they don't deserve and can't understand. Our challenge is to trust that God knows and does what is best in a situation—always. We need to humbly bear in mind that even if we know a great deal, we cannot see the whole picture. We're to ask the all-knowing, all-loving God for the needed wisdom to address life's challenges and accept that we may never understand fully.

Psalms

Setting

Psalms is perhaps the Bible's most beloved book, thanks to its timeless poetry that reflects a wide range of human emotion, including sorrow, elation, love, anger, devotion, fear, and trust. Many of its poems also serve as prayers that express the wonders and challenges of rightly relating to God. Not surprisingly, the psalter has served as a songbook and prayer book for the people of God throughout most of the time of the Bible and beyond.

The 150 psalms (from Greek *psalmos*, "song") were written by many authors over approximately ten centuries. Some date as early as Moses (e.g., Psalm 90, perhaps c. 1400 BC), others as late as after the return from exile (e.g., Psalm 126, c. 400 BC), when the psalter may have reached its final form. Many are anonymous; others were written by Moses and Solomon; nearly half are attributed to David, the musically gifted shepherd (1 Samuel 16:16–23) whom God made king of Israel. Many begin with superscriptions that give one or more of the following details about the psalm: author, occasion, type, and/or the tune to which it was intended to be sung (all the tunes have since been lost). Others give little or no hint to their original setting.

Summary

The book is clearly divided into five parts (1–41; 42–72; 73–89; 90–106; 107–150), but the precise reason for this structure remains unclear, as the sections do not seem organized by author, theme, or time of writing. The five-part form may parallel that of the five books of Moses (Genesis–Deuteronomy), which establish the foundation of God's revelation and explain how his people were originally to relate to him. Certainly the Psalms help God's people continue to relate well to him, and psalms of lament (general complaints about life) predominate at the beginning, while psalms of praise close the book. This pattern may serve to show how we can honestly express our troubles and then move on to praise the good God who governs the world and our lives.

Praise, thanksgiving, and lament are the three main types of psalms. The first expresses admiration for and appreciation to God for who he is and what he has done: "Who is like the LORD our God . . . He raises the poor from the dust" (113:5, 7). The second thanks God for his response to an earlier request: "I sought the LORD, and he answered me" (34:4). And the third, which may be individual or corporate, expresses anguish over some trouble and confidence that God ultimately will deliver: "All my enemies . . . will turn back and suddenly be put to shame" (6:10).

Other types are less common. Some celebrate God's law: "The law of the LORD is perfect, refreshing the soul" (19:7). Some teach wisdom: "Blessed is the one who does not walk in step with the wicked" (1:1). Others magnify God's rule on earth, through the Davidic king in Jerusalem: "I have installed my king on Zion, my holy mountain" (2:6)—or in heaven—"The LORD is King for ever and ever" (10:16). Perhaps the most difficult type for modern readers to appreciate is the imprecatory psalm, wherein the psalmist calls on God to curse his enemies: "Happy is the one who seizes your infants and dashes them against the rocks" (137:9). The enemies of God's people were also God's enemies.

Whatever the type, psalms often use figures of speech to convey their message. A comparison might be explicit—"The wicked . . . are *like* chaff" (1:4)—or implicit: "The Lord *is* my shepherd" (23:1). The modern reader is well served by slowing down and reflecting on what such images are conveying: "like chaff" suggests that the wicked and their works do not hold up when tested by trouble; their acts are as transient as the light husks that encase kernels of grain, which blow away in the breeze. The Psalms also use hyperbole to express strong emotion: "All night long I flood my bed with weeping and drench my couch with tears" (6:6). This may express truth, but not literally—such is the beauty of poetry and the challenge to interpret it properly. Still other poetic devices, like word plays and acrostics (in which successive lines begin with successive letters of the alphabet) are evident in the original Hebrew, even if they don't translate into English.

Significance

God Created and Commands the World

In contrast to the beliefs of all those around them, the Israelites acknowledged a singular God who made and rules the entire world. In the psalms, they recognized that he created all that exists and that he directs it toward his good desired ends, although limited and sinful people like them may struggle to fathom and submit to his sovereignty.

God Had a Covenantal Relationship With Israel

The Creator had especially chosen and bound himself in covenant to the people of Israel, who struggled to live out that relationship appropriately. Their sinfulness often disrupted the relationship; God was willing to forgive, but he expected them to respond in obedience to his revealed commands. The psalmists were sometimes unsure whether they were in right standing with him or of how to obey as they should. In addition, the difficulties they faced often didn't seem to line up with a good God's sovereign control. They wrestled to match their experience with their theology.

God Will Bring the World to a Glorious End

Although life presents difficulties to all people, God's people of the time knew he would ultimately direct the world to its rightful end—with God ruling the world and all peoples finally living in harmony and righteousness both with God and with one another. Until then, they recognized the need to live in harmony with God both individually and corporately, obeying and worshiping him alone.

Contemporary believers relate to God through a different theological framework than did the ancient Israelites, yet the goals and challenges remain largely the same. God made and directs the world, yet we create turmoil with him and with others because of our sin. God forgives our sins, and our challenge is to obey him as he deserves. We can pray and sing the Psalms and so unite with believers through all time and around the world in expressing our joys and sorrows, failures and victories to our good and Sovereign God.

Proverbs

Setting

The book of Proverbs is a work of wisdom literature, written to teach God's people the skill of living well so that one's life produces good results. Unlike the more philosophical wisdom books of Job and Ecclesiastes, most of Proverbs teaches through individual proverbs—memorable statements of two to three lines with practical, general truths about life. The book is cast as a wise older man teaching a younger man how to successfully navigate life by stressing the type of character and behavior that helps one to thrive.

Proverbs is made up of several collections of speeches and proverbs composed by various people. The primary author, the great King Solomon (1:1), was renowned for his wisdom and wrote more than three thousand proverbs (1 Kings 4:29–34). Collections of his proverbs make up major sections of the book (10:1–22:16; 25:1–29:27, and perhaps 1:8–9:18). Another collection is attributed to authors called "the wise" (22:17–24:34), while a few were written by Agur (30:1–33) and King Lemuel (31:1–9), both of whom are otherwise unknown. And some sections are anonymous (1:1–7; 31:10–31).

The book in its entirety was apparently compiled at some point after all its authors wrote the sections attributed to them. The heart of the writings would date to the tenth century BC reign of Solomon, during Israel's golden age, when the writing of literature seemed to flourish. Other parts were likely written later (see 25:1, c. eighth/seventh centuries BC). The book may have reached its final form toward the end of Old Testament history.

Summary

Among the distinct parts of Proverbs are the brief introduction (1:1–7), a section of discourses about the value of wisdom (1:8–9:18), a large section of individual proverbs (10:1–31:9), and finally, an ode to the quintessential virtuous woman (31:10–31).

The introduction names Solomon as the primary author and explains that the book will teach its readers how to understand life and how to live well. It says wisdom and knowledge begin with the fear of the Lord (1:7)—the reverence and awe due the Almighty God. This kind of reverence leads to wise and righteous living, the main subject for the rest of the book.

The next section (1:8–9:18) is a series of extended speeches about wisdom, again depicting an older man addressing a younger man or son, a classic pattern in wisdom literature. Some personify Wisdom as a woman urging the young and naïve to pursue her in order to avoid falling into the destructive ways of evil and sexually immoral people. Hearers who do attain such wisdom generally enjoy a long, secure, and fruitful life.

The longest section (10:1–31:9) contains several collections of individual, seemingly random proverbs written by various authors. These address such themes as speech, marriage and family, work, and self-control. The proverbs often contrast the paths of the wise and the foolish, with widely differing results. A few express absolute truths, describing God and his unchanging character: "The Lord detests those whose hearts are perverse, but he delights in those whose ways are blameless" (11:20). Most give general insights on the way life is; some offer contrasting principles (26:4–5). Such maxims must be interpreted in light of overall biblical teaching, and the wise person will apply them discriminately.

The book closes with a poem in praise of a woman of noble character (31:10–31) whose wisdom, skill, and hard work bring blessing to her family and to others. This portrayal challenges wise young women to emulate her and wise young men to marry a woman on the path to becoming like her.

Significance

Living Well Requires Skill

Proverbs concedes that life is complex, difficult, and sometimes inconsistent, and that one needs skill to successfully negotiate life's unending challenges. The Bible calls this needed skill "wisdom," which Proverbs teaches we can acquire if we acknowledge its source, diligently seek it, and make decisions according to it.

God Knows Best How Life Works

Where does wisdom come from? Attaining it begins with acknowledging that God made the world and knows best how life works. Thus, the wise person doesn't rely on his or her own understanding of what to do but rather seeks to learn what God has revealed. Wisdom requires the humility to accept and admit that God knows infinitely more than we do and we need to live the way that he directs.

Genuine understanding of life and true success always starts with respect for the sovereign God who created all that exists and designed everything. The wise individual learns God's perspective on life and makes decisions according to his principles. These people will find that life is blessed and ultimately satisfying.

Ecclesiastes

Setting

Ecclesiastes, another work of wisdom literature, is philosophical, addressing exceptions to the general truths Proverbs teaches about life. Most of the book is written in a dark, pessimistic tone, arguing that life is often confusing, difficult, and in the end, meaningless—apart from a right relationship with God.

Jewish and Christian traditions ascribe authorship to Solomon, largely because the book describes the writer as the "son of David, king in Jerusalem" (1:1). Yet it never names Solomon, and "son" could also mean a later descendant, including any of Judah's kings (e.g., "son of David" is used even of Jesus—Matthew 1:1), and the form of Hebrew used appears to be a later style than that of Solomon's day. Still, the author's comments about his wisdom, wealth, and accomplishments fit well with the rest of Scripture's portrayal of Solomon. He is the likely author, writing as an older man who learned too late that life lived apart from God is unsatisfying.

Summary

Ecclesiastes opens by introducing its author and theme (1:1–11), gives its mostly bleak perspective on life in two sections (1:12–11:6; 11:7–12:7), and closes with a return to the theme and its more hopeful concluding advice (12:8–14).

The "Teacher" (also translated "Preacher") evidently taught an assembly of people, and he immediately states the oft-repeated mantra: "All is vanity," or "Life is meaningless." Though true in one sense, the point is exaggerated, another trait of the book. Clearly life is not totally meaningless, even if it sometimes appears so, and elsewhere the author makes positive statements about life that also are true. Like many such conflicting teachings in wisdom literature, a wise person discerns which is applicable for a given situation (cf. 3:1–8).

The heart of the book is divided into two parts, both of which present a mostly pessimistic outlook. In 1:12–11:6, the Teacher argues that life is difficult and seems meaningless, but acknowledges that it is a gift from God nonetheless. He had sought meaning in work, pleasure, wealth, wisdom, and power but found nothing truly satisfying. He contends that the certainties of injustice and the inevitability of death make life an insolvable puzzle. (The Teacher lived and wrote before the revelation we now have in the New Testament, so he could not understand fully how, for example, in the afterlife God will right wrongs and reconcile inequities.) But he acknowledges that God has made us so that we can enjoy food and drink, work and possessions, and relationships. He says the wise person should take pleasure in these, realizing that life is a gift from God and should be enjoyed as much as possible. Similarly, verses 11:7 through 12:7 point out that old age and its physical challenges will come, so wise people should enjoy their youth, bearing in mind that in the end God will hold them accountable for their actions.

This last truth fits with the conclusion (12:8–14), which claims that since nothing in life fully satisfies, a wise person will know and obey God, the final judge of all.

Significance

Life Without God Does Not Ultimately Satisfy

This book teaches that most things fail to provide satisfaction and meaning and that life is often difficult and painful. The New Testament likewise affirms that the world is fundamentally flawed because of the corruption of sin—*but* it guarantees that when the time is right God will renew the world (Romans 8:19–21). Until that welcome day, we would do well to follow the advice of Ecclesiastes to "fear God and keep his commandments, for this is the duty of all mankind" (12:13).

Human Wisdom Is Limited, Even for the Godly

Although God is in charge of the world, his reasons for directing some things as he does may be indecipherable even for those who know him. When we reach the limits of our understanding, we must trust that the all-knowing, all-powerful God continues to do what he knows is best.

Since sometimes life is (or at least feels) empty, flawed, and downright incomprehensible, wisdom dictates that we accept our limitations and embrace the knowledge that God both knows what's best and will accomplish it. We should be patient through difficulties and enjoy life's pleasures, bearing in mind that we live before the Lord, and in the end, we will stand before him and give an account of our lives.

Song of Solomon

Setting

The Song of Solomon contains beautiful, highly figurative, often erotic love poetry about the relationship between an Israelite man and woman. The poetic nature of the work and the inherent difficulties in interpreting such historically and culturally distant verse make the Song of Songs one of the most difficult biblical books for today's reader to understand.

The book is clearly associated with Solomon (named in 1:1 and elsewhere), who wrote 1,005 songs (1 Kings 4:32), perhaps including this one. The opening attribution ("Solomon's Song of Songs") could also mean "about Solomon" or "dedicated to Solomon," as well as "authored by." In addition, Solomon's poor example of marital commitment (1 Kings 11:1–8) leads many to disqualify him as a worthy author for a scriptural treatment of love. However, his father, David, also had notorious failures, and it's clear he wrote scores of inspired psalms. Plus, the rabbinic tradition that Solomon wrote the Song as a young man, Proverbs while middle-aged, and Ecclesiastes as an old man could offer a solution to this conundrum: Perhaps he wrote it before his grievous relational missteps.

At any rate, the Song presents numerous interpretive challenges. Plainly it is love poetry, but is it comprised of many largely disconnected poems, or does it tell a coherent story about a relationship progressing from courtship to wedding to maturing union? If it does tell such a story, does it describe three people (Solomon loving a country maiden who loves a country shepherd) or two people (Solomon, also described as a shepherd, loving a country maiden)? Such interpretive difficulties, combined with the book's erotic nature, have led many to interpret the Song as an allegory—an extended figure of speech depicting God's love for Israel (or Christ's love for the church or for individual believers). While a loving marriage certainly illustrates God's love for his people (Hosea 3; Ephesians 5:21–33), the Song most naturally reads as an extended poem about two human lovers (Solomon and a country maiden), and this likely is the correct interpretation.

Summary

Assuming the work does describe Solomon's growing relationship with a young woman, it divides into four sections: courtship (1:1–3:5); wedding and wedding night (3:6–5:1); deepening togetherness, which includes resolving conflict and increasing sexual freedom (5:2–8:4); and a conclusion about the power and source of such love (8:5–14).

The first two sections clearly reflect the man's and woman's desire for each other—both to enjoy each other's presence and to enjoy physical intimacy—which they check through admirable restraint ("Do not arouse or awaken love until it so desires" [2:7]). After the wedding, when they need no longer hold back, they give full expression to their physical desires. The lover praises the beauty and character of his beloved in erotic yet tasteful figures of speech. Even those that sound strange to today's reader ("Your breasts are . . . like twin fawns of a gazelle" [4:5]) must have communicated well in their culture, probably using associations of quality rather than appearance (e.g., fawns = soft and inviting).

The last two sections reflect the reality of marital conflict as well as increasing sexual freedom that is fostered in a healthy relationship. Conflict is portrayed as a dream in which the woman fails to appreciate the man and he draws away; they must restore their closeness by renewing their appreciation for each other. Deepened sexual intimacy follows, now initiated by the woman as well as the man. The conclusion notes that such love comes from God ("the very flame of the LORD" [8:6 ESV]) and in part results when a couple guards their sexual purity before they are married.

Significance

The Song of Solomon shows that sexual intimacy is one of God's greatest gifts and is best enjoyed within an exclusive marital relationship between a man and a woman.

Sex Is a Gift From God

An entire book of the Bible dedicated to love, marriage, and sexual pleasure shows that God created humans so that we can experience these, including the physical and emotional intimacy sex provides. Even though humans often corrupt this gift, God intended it to be a delight and wants us to enjoy it abundantly.

Sexual Intimacy Is Best Within Marriage

The book teaches that sex is best enjoyed within the borders of marriage. An exclusive, lifelong relationship between man and woman represents God's design (Genesis 2:24) and the optimum setting for delighting in this powerful creation. This was true three thousand years ago and is no less true today.

No matter how people misuse or corrupt it, Christians should not think badly of this divine gift; rather, we ought to redeem and embrace it. To find in it the delight and closeness God wants us to have, let us reserve sex for marriage and then keep that relationship exclusive, continually growing in its intimacy.

Isaiah

Setting

Isaiah is a classic Old Testament prophetic book with messages of judgment and restoration for the nation of Judah, dynamic fore-tellings of the life and ministry of Jesus, and an exalted portrayal of the holy God who is sovereign over the world and over history.

The book clearly identifies its author as Isaiah (1:1), who ministered for some sixty years in the eighth and seventh centuries (740–681) BC. However, there is some question as to whether he wrote the entire book because of markedly different tones and settings for its three major parts. The harsher material in chapters 1 through 39 warns Judah of forthcoming judgment; it is set during the Assyrian threat against Judah during the lifetime of Isaiah, who's frequently named in this section. The rest of the book, on the other hand, does not mention Isaiah and is more positive in tone; it is set during the Babylonian exile (40–55; sixth century BC) and the restoration under the Persians (56–66; fifth century BC).

While some say a later writer (or writers) must have written chapters 40 through 66, the work nowhere names another author, and New Testament writers frequently quote from its various parts as written by Isaiah (e.g., Jesus, in John 12:38, 40 quoting Isaiah 6 and Isaiah 53). Each major part also includes characteristic phrases such as *Holy One of Israel* and *high and exalted* to describe God, likewise suggesting one author—Isaiah—who wrote in the eighth and seventh centuries about his day as well as about what God would do in the future.

Summary

The book divides neatly into the three parts described above. The first section (1–39) can further subdivide into three subsections (1–12; 13–35; 36–39). In chapters 1 through 12, Isaiah warns that God will judge Judah for its sins but also offers the hope of restoration for a purified remnant from among the people. Chapters 13 through 35 expand the warnings of God's judgment to apply to nations like Babylon, Assyria, Philistia, and Egypt. They aren't covenantal partners with God, as Israel is, but he still holds them accountable. Chapters 36 through 39 contain primarily narrative material that transitions from the Assyrian period (1–35) to the later Babylonian period, the setting for the next section.

This first main section (1–39) focuses on Judean kings to show the results of both unsuitable and suitable trust in God. Ahaz (Isaiah 7; c. 735 BC) fails to trust God when facing a crucial threat from both neighboring Israel and also Syria; he earns God's rebuke in response. Hezekiah (Isaiah 36–37; 701 BC) does trust God when facing an even greater threat, from Assyria, and Jerusalem is saved as a result.

The second main section (40–55) shifts from the threat of harsh judgment to the bright hope of restoration, beginning with "Comfort, comfort my people, says your God. Speak tenderly to Jerusalem, and proclaim to her . . . that her sin has been paid for" (40:1–2). After exiling Judah to Babylon, God promises to restore his people through his servant(s), identified variously as Israel

(44:21), the Persian king Cyrus (45:13), and an unnamed suffering servant (52:13–53:12), whom multiple New Testament writers later identify clearly as Jesus.

The third main section (56–66) illustrates that Judah's restoration from exile would continue during the period of Persian rule. At this time, corrupt leaders, insincere worship, and continued idolatry will persistently demonstrate the ongoing need for the Messiah, who would come several centuries later.

Significance

God Judges and Restores His People When Needed

As do many Old Testament prophetic books, Isaiah warns the Judean people and Davidic kings that they are in danger of judgment for failing to remain faithful to the Mosaic covenant. At first they can avoid judgment if they repent; when they do not, judgment through conquerors like Assyria or Babylon becomes inevitable. That certainty is tempered by the equal certainty that afterward God will restore Judah to its homeland, although only a purified remnant will survive to experience it. Christians today relate to God under a different covenant (the new rather than the Mosaic), yet still we can be sure that God judges and restores us when and how he knows we need it.

God Knows and Controls History

The God who pledged to bring down and then raise up Judah could do so because he knew and superintended history, ever directing it toward his desired end. As he knew events before they happened, he could foretell them through his prophets. Through Isaiah (7:14) he said a maiden (also translated "virgin") would conceive and give birth to a son and call him Immanuel—fulfilled by the virgin birth of Jesus. God also predicted the name of the

Persian king Cyrus 150 years before he lived (44:28), and described the suffering of Jesus seven centuries in advance (52:13–53:12). God's ownership of history ultimately led to raising up the Messiah, David's final heir, to make possible salvation for all people.

God Expects His People to Trust Him

The all-knowing and sovereign God expected his people to trust his control of national and world events and to believe he knew what was best for them individually. Their failure to do so and remain faithful according to their covenant showed that for the most part they did not trust him. Some, like King Hezekiah, did trust and witnessed the Lord's miraculous deliverance.

The same God who expected the Judeans of Isaiah's day to trust him likewise expects this faith of his people today. God knows how history will play out for our world, our nation, and our lives; we must trust that he's doing what's best for us, corporately and individually.

Jeremiah

Setting

This book contains prophetic messages given through—and intriguing narrative about—Jeremiah, who served as God's primary prophetic voice during the terrible days when Babylon threatened and then conquered Judah (626–586 BC; Jeremiah 1:2), much like Isaiah had during the Assyrian threat to Judah a century earlier. God called Jeremiah, a sensitive man and a priest from a small village a few miles north of Jerusalem, to a challenging ministry that would earn him the title of "the weeping prophet." He faithfully warned the obstinate Judeans that God would bring harsh judgment if they did not repent of their idolatry, but he faced such opposition and saw so little response that he could only weep for the suffering he knew would come (9:1).

Jeremiah's ministry began during the reign of Josiah, Judah's last godly king, whose death ended any hope of the nation avoiding judgment, as subsequent kings incurred the wrath of God and then of Babylon through their foolish and wicked actions. On top of the poetic messages of judgment and restoration, the prose accounts of Jeremiah's ministry include symbolic portrayals of

God's messages. After exile, God *will* restore a remnant and make a new covenant—and Jesus himself *will* eventually inaugurate it.

Summary

While the overall themes are clear, the book's organization is not. The rather chaotic arrangement may well reflect the tumultuous times endured by Jeremiah and Baruch, his scribe and partner who likely wrote down and compiled (36:4–8) much of it.

Chapter 1 introduces Jeremiah, the dates of his ministry, and his call to prophesy. It follows with a vision that illustrates two major themes. First, God will judge Judah through a nation invading from the north (Babylon). Second, God commands Jeremiah to deliver these grim messages and promises to protect him in the face of great persecution.

Jeremiah's ministry and Judah's final pre-exile years unfold through chapters 2 through 39. He charges the Judeans with violating their covenant with God and urges them to repent. When they refuse, he guarantees that God will judge them through Babylon's rising power. In chapters 30 through 33, God promises to deliver the Judeans after judgment, in part through the new covenant (discussed below). Chapters 34 through 39 contain stories of how the promised judgment plays out in Judah, including the fall of the capital, Jerusalem.

Chapters 40 through 52 close the book and the ministry of Jeremiah. Chapters 40 through 45 describe events after Jerusalem's fall, when a group of Jews rebel against the new government set up by the Babylonians and flee to Egypt for safety, forcing Jeremiah to accompany them (perhaps in hopes that God would then protect them). Chapters 46 through 51 tell of God's judgment on foreign nations as well. Chapter 52 again recounts the fall of Jerusalem— possibly to emphasize Judah's guilt above that of the other nations.

Significance

God Is Patient, but He Eventually Punishes Sin

The God who created and governs the world merits loyalty and obedience from all people, especially from his particular covenantal people. Israel and Judah were most accountable; God kept his promises to judge them through the armies of Assyria and Babylon and to restore a remnant afterward.

Ministry May Be Tough

The prophet Jeremiah faithfully obeyed what God called him to do, but he suffered rejection, beatings, and imprisonment from stubborn people who didn't want to hear what God was saying through him. As his ministry shows, people often refuse to cooperate with God, making life difficult for those who represent him.

God Is Committed to Establishing a Community of Faithful Followers

Jeremiah had to foretell and then witness God's judgment on the people of Judah for their unfaithfulness to their covenant. He also announced that God would restore a community of faithful followers afterward, in part by establishing the new covenant (31:31–34). Some six hundred years would pass, but at the close of his ministry Jesus would inaugurate that covenant (Luke 22:20), which would be open to *all* people who believe in him.

God calls believers to faithfully fulfill their role in his great work. He took centuries to judge the people's unfaithfulness under the Mosaic covenant, and centuries more to inaugurate the new covenant. Now, some twenty centuries have passed, and God continues to add to his people through those who relate to him through this covenant. We are part of this, and we need to use whatever he has gifted us with and do what he has called us to do.

Lamentations

Setting

The book of Lamentations poetically expresses the anguish of Judean survivors shortly after the Babylonians destroyed Jerusalem and killed or exiled most of its inhabitants (586 BC). God had sent prophet after prophet to warn the people that disloyalty to their covenant with him would result in destruction if they failed to repent; now the painful judgment has come. In Lamentations, they mourn their sin and its consequences.

The book's date and occasion are clear; its authorship is not. Jewish tradition ascribes it to Jeremiah, an eyewitness to the tragedy. However, while the prophet wrote at least one lament (for the dead King Josiah; 2 Chronicles 35:25), Lamentations includes no claim of authorship, and the accounts of Jeremiah's activities after the city's fall (Jeremiah 40–45) nowhere state that he wrote this book. Either he or another theologically sensitive eyewitness wrote it to mourn the Jews' losses, to confess that the judgment was deserved, and to plead with God to show mercy and restore them.

Summary

Lamentations is comprised of laments—similar to those in the Psalms—that express distress because of hardship as well as hope that God will deliver. The five chapters are five laments mourning Jerusalem's destruction; the first four are acrostics, wherein successive lines begin with successive letters of the Hebrew alphabet, a pattern that does not translate into English. Chapters 1, 2, and 4 have twenty-two verses, one for each Hebrew letter, while chapter 3 has sixty-six, with every three lines beginning with successive letters. The effect is literary artistry, expressing the fullness of Jerusalem's suffering "from A to Z." That the last chapter is not an acrostic perhaps emphasizes that something is missing, like a resolution between the Judean people and their God.

Each chapter laments Jerusalem's fall in a slightly different fashion. Chapter 1 describes the city as a mourning widow, deserted, aware that her sin has led to her suffering. Chapter 2 depicts God as a divine warrior who comes in anger to fight against, not for, his people. The much longer chapter 3 portrays Jerusalem as a man suffering, or perhaps counseling the city to repent. In the middle of this lament, the tone turns positive, focused on hope because of God's faithful and gracious character. "Because of the LORD's great love we are not consumed, for his compassions never fail. They are new every morning; great is your faithfulness" (vv. 22–23). In chapter 4, the community mourns the extent of the destruction, and in chapter 5, the community prays for God to remember and restore them.

Significance

Suffering Is Sometimes Deserved

Sometimes suffering comes to those who've done nothing to merit it, but sometimes God's people do suffer deservedly. As with the ancient Judeans of Jeremiah's time, God may justly allow natural pain and suffering due to the sin of his people.

God, Faithful and Compassionate, Is Always Ready to Forgive

No matter the sin, God always offers forgiveness. His faithful and compassionate character means he will *always* forgive when his people truly repent. God invariably offers hope for a new start, even though the consequences of sin may remain, as they did for fallen Jerusalem.

We often suffer hardship not connected to any fault of our own. But when we do suffer because of something for which we're responsible, we need to own that responsibility and confess our wrong. Then we can ask God to forgive us and start anew. Such offerings of confession and requests for mercy are necessary to restore a broken relationship with God. He will always forgive, even if he allows consequences to remain.

Ezekiel

Setting

The book of Ezekiel records God's words to exiled Judeans living in Babylon around the time Jerusalem and the temple were destroyed. God sent messages of judgment and then encouragement through Ezekiel, who'd been exiled with ten thousand others (597 BC; 2 Kings 24:10–14). He'd been born to a priestly family but never worked in that capacity because he was exiled before age thirty, when priests began their service. Instead, God called him to prophesy while in exile (593 BC). Ezekiel ministered for the next twenty years as Judah continued to rebel against God and Babylon and was conquered.

Ezekiel shared what God said with his fellow exiles in both personal and colorful fashion. The book is written entirely in the first person, suggesting Ezekiel as the sole author. He also recounts prophetic visions, acts out symbolic messages, and records narratives of events, all in order to announce God's judgment on Judah and other nations as well as to promise future restoration for the Jews.

Summary

The book breaks into sections arranged around prophetic themes: judgment on Judah and Jerusalem (1–24), judgment on foreign nations (25–32), and the restoration of Judah (33–48).

Chapters 1 through 24 open with an apocalyptic vision* describing God in his heavenly glory, including Ezekiel's call as a prophet. Most of the rest of this section proclaims judgment on the Jews. Of particular note is the vision (chapters 8–11) that records God's departure from the temple because of their sin, especially idolatry. Since the Lord was withdrawing his protective presence, the temple's destruction was inevitable—a particularly poignant message for a priest and prophet to deliver.

In the second section (25–32), Ezekiel conveys guarantees of judgment against nearby and distant nations, including Ammon, Moab, Lebanon, and Egypt. These verdicts show God's sovereignty over the whole world as well as over his particular people, the Jews. Of particular interest is the condemnation of the king of Tyre (28:1–19), the second half of which describes the king's pride and downfall in a way that seems to escalate beyond that of a human being, and actually describes Satan at his original rebellion and fall.

The final section (33–48) describes how God will restore and bless the Jews after he has purified them through judgment. Some messages likely should be seen as figurative rather than literal, as they do not fit the subsequent restoration of the Jews to their land. For example, the description of the restored temple (40–43) does not match the one rebuilt by the returnees from exile or even Herod the Great's more expansive renovation of it around the time of Jesus. Perhaps Ezekiel's vision symbolizes God's presence with his people—fulfilled through Jesus' ministry—rather than describing a literal building. Nonetheless, Ezekiel's prophecies plainly describe

---

*See more on apocalyptic visions under "Summary" in Daniel.

the certainty of God's pouring out abundant blessing on his people by restoring them and renewing their land.

Significance

Tragedies Are Not God's Fault, but They Are Sometimes Deserved

Babylon's conquest of Judah and the destruction of Jerusalem and its temple represent some of the worst tragedies suffered by God's people during their long history. God allowed these events to take place, but he was not to blame; his people were. Their sin brought about judgment, which God used to cleanse and purify them.

God's Restoration Continues in the New Testament and Beyond

Through Ezekiel, God promised both judgment and restoration. Some of that restoration took place by the end of the Old Testament era. More occurred during the New Testament era with the ministry of Jesus, when God literally lived with his people (e.g., Ezekiel 34:23; John 10). And still more restoration continues in events foretold by Ezekiel and in the New Testament that have yet to occur (e.g., Ezekiel 47:1–12; Revelation 22:1–5).

Our lives include difficulties and tragedies, even if not to the extent that the Jews at the time of Ezekiel experienced. If God was sovereign over their tragedies, patiently working them out for good, believers today can trust him to do the same with whatever they face—personally, corporately, and throughout history. God is no less good and sovereign now than he was thousands of years ago.

Daniel

Setting

The book of Daniel contains some of the Bible's most well-known stories as well as some of its most cryptic visions about future events. Both reflect God's control over events during Daniel's day, and they promise his control over events that would befall the Jews in the centuries that followed. Further, all (stories and visions) show that while God allows challenging things to happen, he guides everything to his desired ends, making it possible for his people to experience peace amid distressing circumstances.

The events and visions cover the region's history from the time of Babylonian dominance to that of Roman supremacy. The *events* took place over roughly seventy years, as first Babylon and then Persia rose to overpower the region, with Judah a subjected nation and many Jews exiled to distant lands. The *visions* mostly predict events that would happen over several subsequent centuries, when the Greeks and Romans would likewise take their turns in power.

Daniel himself appears to have written or narrated much of the book, which shows God's control over events and history. Nearly half is in the first person (e.g., "*my* vision . . . *I* looked" [7:2]), and

Jesus himself refers to a prophecy that came "through the prophet Daniel" (Matthew 24:15). An editor after the time of Daniel may have collated the stories and visions. The Jews of Daniel's day endured conquest and exile, and Jews several centuries later would suffer even worse, yet Daniel shows they could trust God's goodness and sovereignty no matter what they faced.

Summary

The book breaks neatly into two halves. The first (1–6) narrates six stories about events that occur during Daniel's time in exile; the second (7–12) records four apocalyptic visions about yet-to-happen events focused on a period four centuries ahead. Both sections reflect God's control despite evil and suffering.

In chapters 1 through 3, Daniel and/or his friends, exiled far from home, proceed to flourish in a pagan land. Chapter 1 introduces the book's major theme: King Nebuchadnezzar sacks Jerusalem, but it was "the Lord [who] delivered [the] king of Judah into his hand" (1:2). Thus, while tragedy comes to Judah, God is still in charge. The Babylonians train Daniel, Shadrach, Meshach, and Abednego as court advisors and try to make them conform to Babylonian thought and faith. However, the exiles stand firm, and God blesses them with health and success.

In chapter 2 an irate Nebuchadnezzar decrees death to his advisors regarding the content and interpretation of a troubling dream about a statue made of four metals. Daniel and friends survive this threat when God gives Daniel the needed information—the statue represented four successive kingdoms that would rule the region—thus demonstrating that God is the true source of knowledge and wisdom. And in chapter 3 the account of Daniel's friends miraculously surviving the blazing furnace clearly reflects God's power to protect his people anywhere, anytime.

Chapters 4 through 6 continue these themes. First, God humbles the proud Nebuchadnezzar, making him live like a beast for seven years until he acknowledges God's superiority. Then God also brings down his successor, the vain and reckless Belshazzar, but rather than repenting, Belshazzar dies, and the kingdom passes to Persian hands. Finally, Daniel's surviving the lions' den, after others plotted to destroy him, shows God's ability to preserve a faithful man from certain death. All six stories emphasize God's sovereignty in the midst of tragedy and his ability to preserve his people even in exile.

In chapters 7 through 12, Daniel recounts four apocalyptic visions from God that show his control over troubles that would befall the Jews in the coming centuries. Apocalyptic visions differ from regular prophecy in several respects. Rather than God's sharing verbal messages through a prophet, apocalyptic visions are made up of vivid, often unnatural imagery, full of elements that represent something else. Regular prophecy urges people to turn from their own evil deeds; apocalyptic prophecy encourages perseverance in the face of external evil until God finally removes or destroys it.

In the first vision, Daniel sees four beasts that represent the same succession of four kingdoms represented by the metals in Nebuchadnezzar's dream. An enthroned God and glorified Son of Man judge these beasts, and in the end God establishes an eternal kingdom. A similar vision of a ram and a goat in chapter 8 represent Persia later being conquered by Greece, plus a later Greek ruler who would fiercely persecute the Jews.

In chapter 9 Daniel prays for God to end the Jews' seventy-year exile; God sends an angel to foretell the Jews' future in a cryptic framework of seventy "sevens" or "weeks," likely an intentionally vague framework of time. God foretells significant future events but apparently finds it unnecessary to explain exactly when these will occur. In Daniel's final vision (10–12), an angel describes the unseen spiritual realm and gives more detailed information about the future, including the coming of a blasphemous ruler who will mercilessly persecute the Jews in the second century BC. God will allow this terrible reality but still deliver the Jews from destruction. Altogether the four visions predict both future troubles and God's sovereignty over what will take place.

Significance

God Is Sovereign Over and Throughout History

By Daniel's time, the nation's dominance in the days of David and Solomon was a distant memory. Now, centuries later, they were dominated by other nations, and plainly they would remain a conquered people for centuries more. Though this oppression was surely not what the people wanted, God was showing that nothing is beyond his control.

God Sometimes Allows Bad Things to Occur

God knows the future and directs history; nothing occurs outside his reach. For his people, in Daniel's day and beyond, the future would include conquest, exile, and terrible persecution. God can miraculously rescue his people from fire and lions, but he doesn't always. Sometimes, in his infinite wisdom, he permits real harm to his people, and he doesn't always tell us why.

God's People Can Trust His Sovereignty

Those who believe and follow the Lord need to trust that when he allows anything that is not or does not seem good to us, he can use it for ultimately good ends. This knowledge should provide God's people with peace and comfort in the face of anything that confronts them. Evil has not yet been finally and forever banished, and it won't be until after the Messiah comes for the second time.

If God was working events out as was best for Daniel and the Jews during the hardships of that day as well as in the years that followed, we today can trust that God likewise knows all of our situations and works through our circumstances for our good. He doesn't guarantee his people an easy road, but he does promise to be with us through whatever he allows to come our way.

Hosea

Setting

Using one of the most powerful illustrations in the entire Bible, the book of Hosea tells how God orders the prophet to marry a woman who would be unfaithful to him, thus portraying how Israel had been unfaithful to their God. Some interpreters find the command morally offensive and argue that the story must be figurative, not literal. However, because nothing in the Old Testament forbids a prophet from marrying such a person, the story likely is historical, and is a potent example of the infidelity lived out by God's people.

The book is set at the time when the northern kingdom of Israel was nearing—and then enduring—conquest and exile at the hands of the brutal Assyrians (c. 750–715 BC). It tells of Hosea's tragic marriage, and then gives a series of prophetic messages of warning and judgment. Hosea himself apparently wrote the book to his contemporary Israelites, using the figurative and poetic style typically found in Hebrew prophecy.

Summary

The book's first section (1–3) tells of the prophet Hosea, who obeys God's challenging command to marry Gomer, a woman he knows will commit adultery. Later, Hosea again obeys God and gives his children names like "not loved" and "not my people" to illustrate God's painful but temporary rejection and judgment of Israel. Hosea's gracious restoration of his relationship with his estranged wife exemplifies God's promise to graciously restore his relationship with the nation.

The other section (4–14) gives a series of messages apparently delivered by Hosea during his long ministry. These warn the Israelites that God will surely judge them for covenantal violations like idolatry, but also promise that in the end he will restore them. Numerous metaphors illustrate the people's infidelity and God's grace in overcoming their unfaithfulness.

Significance

God Uses Obedient Followers in Powerful Ways

"When the LORD began to speak through Hosea, the LORD said to him, 'Go, marry a promiscuous woman.'" Hosea obeyed this as well as God's further commands, such as the names he gave to his children. His willingness to do whatever God asked made it possible for God to use him in powerful ways.

Gracious People Can Restore Even Deeply Fractured Relationships

Just as God would restore his badly damaged relationship with Israel, Hosea restores his deeply fractured marriage with his wife. How? First, he speaks kindly to her in private (2:14) to begin the process of restoration. Then he exhibits grace by forgiving her, far beyond what her actions merit (3:1). Such love elicits a positive response from her, just as Israel would need to respond to God; as the offending party, Israel must confess its offense (14:1–2). These situations illustrate how broken relationships can be restored—even in cases of grievous offense—when the offender admits the wrong committed and the offended offers forgiveness.

For now, in this world, relationships become torn both between people and between people and God. When we're involved in such a failure, God calls us to admit our offense and/or to offer undeserved grace. If we obey this call, he can use us as his instruments in a world that is badly in need of healing.

Joel

Setting

In the book of Joel, the prophet uses a devastating locust plague to warn disobedient Judah about a potentially worse problem: God's impending judgment. Since the book does not name contemporary kings—the normal way of dating in that era—the precise historical context is unclear. If Joel is anticipating judgment through Babylon's conquest, as seems likely, he may have spoken and written the book shortly before that (586 BC).

Summary

Joel first (1:1–20) describes the effects of a plague coupled with drought that, together, were destroying the crops and pastureland of agriculturally based Judah. These curses for not obeying God (Deuteronomy 28:15–23) spell disaster for everyone—even for the priests, who rely on offerings that people can no longer give. Joel warns that this prefigures a greater coming tragedy (Joel 2:1–17), when God will use an invading army to judge his people. They can escape only through true repentance: "Rend your heart and not your garments" (v. 13). If they do, God will relent and restore them (2:18–3:21) by allowing the land to heal, protecting them from invaders, and pouring out his Spirit to save all who turn to him.

Significance

God Acts and Offers Salvation to All

Joel often speaks of "the day of the LORD"—the time when God would act to make things right. The Jews had thought that "day" would involve God judging others and elevating them; actually, Joel warns, this judgment would start with his people. God's promised restoration (2:28–29) would eventually include offering his Spirit in salvation to all peoples, including Gentiles as well as Jews (Acts 2:17–21).

God acts in history to bring about his purposes. When we, his people, are obedient, we can look forward to his acting in redeeming ways. If we are disobedient, his action may in fact be our discipline.

Amos

Setting

In this book God uses Amos, a herdsman and farmer from Judah, to judge the northern kingdom of Israel. With no formal prophetic training (7:14), Amos obediently prophesies against the wealthy and corrupt Israelites, apparently during a temporary decline in Assyrian power (c. 750 BC) that has allowed Israel to expand and flourish. Its prosperity has come in part from exploitation of the poor. Amos predicts, and later writes, that God will judge them for this and other breaches of their covenant with him.

Summary

Amos has three sections. The first (1–2) conveys judgment against foreign nations, mostly for military crimes. The sequence then narrows to focus on Israel, whom God promises to judge not for war crimes but for violating its covenant. The second section (3–6) continues these messages of judgment wherein, as in a lawsuit, God charges and finds Israel guilty, especially of social injustice. The final section (7–9) includes four visions: Amos gets God to relent from sending locusts and fire, but not to indefinitely forestall judgment. Then, a builder's plumb line and a basket of fruit symbolize that Israel is crooked (unrighteous) and ripe for judgment. Thankfully, the book ends with a hopeful message of God's promise for future restoration.

Significance

God Is Just; We Must Not Ignore Social Injustice

The messages he gives through Amos demonstrate that God requires right actions from all nations and that his people are most responsible to follow his commands and to treat others well, especially the poor.

As God's people, we must know that he holds us to the highest standard of conduct. Should he bless us with wealth and power, we are to use it not to mistreat others but to bless them, reflecting and expressing his special concern for the poor and the powerless.

Obadiah

Setting

The brief book of Obadiah announces God's judgment against the neighboring nation of Edom for its harsh treatment of crippled Judah. It ends with God's pledge to restore Judah, which God had punished with Babylon's conquest (586 BC). Through Obadiah, apparently prophesying shortly afterward, God promises that despite their security (the land of Edom could be defended with ease), he will destroy the Edomites completely.

Summary

The book's twenty-one verses break into three sections: judgment, reason for judgment, and contrasting restoration. God promises thorough judgment on Edom (vv. 1–9), from which it will not recover. The Edomites deserve this (vv. 10–16) for their mistreatment of the Judeans in the latter's downfall: they had rejoiced at Judah's misfortune when Babylon conquered it, they had taken Judean territory, and they had killed escapees. In contrast to this final judgment of Edom, God eventually will restore the chastised Judeans and give them dominion (vv. 17–21).

Significance

Do Not Gloat When an Enemy Falls

Although the Edomites were enemies of the Judeans, the two peoples were also related (descendants of Isaac's sons Esau and Jacob, respectively). Edom should have aided Judah in its distress instead of rejoicing and helping in its destruction. No matter how seemingly justifiable, gloating over a foe's misfortune is wrong.

God's Promises Are Always Fulfilled

Just as God promised, he thoroughly judged Edom and restored Judah, though he waited many centuries to fulfill it. The Edomite people disappeared into history; by contrast, more than six million Jews now live in reestablished Israel alone.

God's people today also must beware of rejoicing when an enemy stumbles; he calls us to demonstrate kindness, not vengeance (Matthew 5:43–48). We likewise can trust that he will carry out all his promises in due time.

Jonah

Setting

The book of Jonah tells of an Israelite prophet who reluctantly obeys God's command to preach to an enemy people, only to object when God shows them mercy. Given the information in the book, Jonah must have written it or perhaps conveyed much of it to another author. Jonah's home was Gath Hepher, a village in Galilee, and his ministry dates to the mid-eighth century BC (2 Kings 14:25), when the Israelites were prospering.

Jonah's story includes his amazing adventure in the belly of a whale, leading some to ask whether the story is an allegory or parable and not an actual event. However, the account, longer and more detailed than biblical parables, reads much like the historical narratives of the prophets Elijah and Elisha (1 and 2 Kings). In addition, documented examples of people surviving after being swallowed by whales* argue for the story's plausibility, and Jesus' reference to Jonah's ordeal (Matthew 12:39–41) argues for its historicity (even though one could refer to a known fictional event

*"The Sign of the Prophet Jonah and Its Modern Confirmations," *Princeton Theological Review* 25 (1927): 636–637.

to make a valid comparison). Regardless, Jonah's story highlights God's compassion for unbelievers and the importance of living in line with his purposes rather than working against what he is doing.

Summary

The story divides into halves, each told in two chapters. In the first, God commands Jonah to warn the Assyrian city of Nineveh about impending judgment. Instead, the Israelite prophet literally goes in the opposite direction in a failed attempt to escape his appointed task. His reluctance to help is understandable, given the Assyrians' known cruelty and their intent to conquer the lands along the eastern Mediterranean, including Israel. But God does not excuse Jonah's disobedience and sends a storm that endangers everyone on the small ship Jonah has boarded in his effort to flee. In contrast to the prophet running from God, the sea, and the storm, even the unbelieving sailors immediately obey God; Jonah is cast into the sea to get his attention and move him to repent.

A whale (literally, "large fish") obeys God's command as well and swallows the prophet, who does repent and offers a prayer of thanksgiving for his rescue. The whale then obeys God once more and spits the chastened Jonah onto dry land.

The book's second half records Jonah's obedience to God's repeated call and then his miserable attitude when God shows mercy to the Ninevites. Jonah journeys perhaps seven hundred miles to the enormous city and warns its inhabitants that due to their sin God will judge them if they will not repent. Assyrian annals mention a plague, a long revolt, and a solar eclipse during 765–759 BC, perhaps just before Jonah's time, and God may have used these to prepare the audience for his message. Whatever the reason, the Ninevites repent wholeheartedly, and God shows mercy by not destroying the city.

But the story doesn't end there. Jonah grows angry that God spares the city, and God again uses nature to pique the disobedient Israelite. God provides a plant to shade Jonah from the hot sun, then sends a worm to kill the plant. Sadly, Jonah actually cares more for the plant than for the 120,000 inhabitants of Nineveh! The book concludes with God using a rhetorical question to rebuke Jonah and emphasize the importance of showing compassion to people—which Jonah obviously has failed to do.

Significance

God Cares for Outsiders

God cared for the Ninevites and expected his prophet to do so as well. Probably like the other Israelites of his day, Jonah did not care for them and, from a human perspective, had a good reason not to: The Assyrians, known for malicious cruelty, had threatened Israel in the recent past. Nevertheless, Jonah's lack of compassion showed how the Israelites had become self-centered and insensitive to God's concern for other peoples.

God Controls the World, but Not Always His People

Throughout the story, aspects of nature as well as non-Israelite people respond well to God's commands: the sea, the storm, the sailors, the whale, the Ninevite king and his subjects, the plant, and the worm. By contrast, the Israelite prophet almost always disobeys God, or obeys reluctantly and with a bad attitude. Jonah becomes hardhearted and does not fulfill his calling. The people of Israel likewise become hardhearted and disobedient and don't do what God requires of them: obey his commands and reflect his character to outsiders.

Just as the callous, selfish, defiant Israelite prophet and his people failed to fulfill God's call on them, so believers today sometimes neglect God's call. We may indeed have seemingly good reasons for what we want or don't want to occur in certain situations. But if we aren't obeying God or aren't reflecting his character toward others, God may allow us to be "thrown overboard" with some type of discipline to get our attention and give us the opportunity to respond better.

Micah

Setting

In this book, Micah (a contemporary of Isaiah and Hosea) warns the Israelites in the late eighth and early seventh century BC that God will scatter them in judgment, but later restore them. The name *Micah* means "Who is like Yahweh?" and reflects the prophet's challenge for his audience to consider their incomparable God and respond with loyal worship and service.

Summary

Micah contains two cycles (1–5; 6–7) of messages about judgment and restoration.

In the first, chapters 1 through 3 warn of judgment, beginning with Micah calling on God to testify in a figurative lawsuit against Israel and Judah for their failures. The nations' leaders—prophets, priests, and political figures—are particularly accountable for the rampant idolatry, economic corruption, and violence. Chapters 4 through 5 promise future restoration, when Jerusalem's temple will serve as the center of worship for many peoples and God will bless his people with peace and prosperity. Part of the fulfillment would come through a ruler who Micah famously foretells will be born in Bethlehem (5:2).

The second cycle (6–7) also opens with a legal dispute between God and his people and closes with a pledge of salvation. Israel's matchless God forgives and shows mercy.

Significance

God Judges, and God Forgives

As with the people of Israel and Judah in Micah's day, even when God disciplines us, he forgives and restores us when we repent and turn to him. We're to obey him and rely on him, allowing his Spirit to work in us to make us more and more like him. In this way we're increasingly able to reflect his character, showing justice and mercy to others and humbly living in fellowship with him (6:8).

Nahum

Setting

In the book of Nahum God promises to bring down Nineveh, the capital of Assyria, which long had been his people's brutal oppressor. Known for its military prowess and exceptional cruelty, Assyria threatened the northern (Israel) and southern (Judah) kingdoms for more than two centuries before conquering Israel (732–722 BC) and then nearly finishing off Judah in 701 BC. Now God promises vengeance, which will mean relief for Judah.

An otherwise unknown prophet named Nahum wrote this book sometime between the Assyrian conquest of Thebes in Egypt (664 BC; 3:8–10) and Nineveh's fall (612 BC) during the decline of the once-mighty Assyrian empire.

Summary

The book includes several messages of judgment against Nineveh and of deliverance for Judah. Chapter 1 describes God as a divine warrior who will destroy Nineveh but restore Judah. In chapter 2 Nahum describes the future battle at Nineveh and compares the city to a den of lions. Chapter 3 says it will fall just as surely as Thebes had fallen to Assyria.

Significance

God Sets Things Right—In His Time

Assyria had harassed the northern and southern kingdoms for centuries before its forces conquered Israel and wielded massive destruction upon Judah. *Now* God will take vengeance on this oppressor. Even if he waits what seems a very long time while certain elements play out as he knows best, the Lord's justice is certain and thorough.

When believers today ask God to right some injustice, we can be confident that he will act—but in his time and in his way, not ours. We must accept that God may wait much longer than we would like to right the wrong and bring about justice.

Habakkuk

Setting

This book records a conversation between God and Habakkuk in which the prophet voices two complaints. First, he protests that God is not acting to punish sin in Judah. Then, when God says he will judge the sin, the prophet complains about *how* God intends to do it. Ultimately, Habakkuk accepts God's plan as best.

The date of this dialogue is unclear, but since Babylon's future rise seems to surprise Habakkuk, it may date between 626 BC, when Babylon begins ascending, and 605 BC, when it sacks Jerusalem (and by which time Judah is exceedingly corrupt).

Summary

The book begins with the prophet's complaint that God has not been judging sin in Judah, to which God says he will send Babylon as his instrument of judgment. Habakkuk expresses surprise and dismay; surely the Babylonians are more evil than the Judeans. God guarantees that eventually he will judge the Babylonians as well, and in the end Habakkuk expresses trust in God's way, despite how much it means Judah will suffer.

Significance

God Knows Best, Even When His People Suffer

Like Habakkuk, those who follow the Lord suffer from the evil in their society. God's plan to use the Babylonians, which will lead to conquest and exile, means more suffering. Eventual restoration, after Babylon is judged, will not come for generations. Habakkuk's response? "Yet I will wait patiently . . . yet I will rejoice in the LORD" (3:16, 18). He accepts that God's plan is best even if it includes great difficulty over much time.

Believers today also need to accept how God works, including how he deals with problems, even if we sometimes don't like it. We need to live out Habakkuk 2:4: "The righteous shall live by his faith" (ESV). Paul twice quotes this verse in the New Testament (Romans 1:17; Galatians 3:11) to emphasize that *a person becomes righteous through faith*; originally, Habakkuk means that *one who is righteous must live in faith*, trusting that God will work things out as he knows to be best. Both should be true of us.

Zephaniah

Setting

The book of Zephaniah announces God's judgment on Judah as well as on other nations, but promises that a purified remnant will survive. Zephaniah prophesies during the reign of Josiah, Judah's last good king. Josiah led a religious reform beginning in 621 BC, yet its effects did not outlast his death (609 BC). Zephaniah's preaching also addresses many of Josiah's concerns, suggesting that the prophet's words may have supported the king's efforts. Sadly, most Judeans do not heed these calls to repent, and the nation heads toward the predicted judgment.

Summary

Zephaniah splits into three sections: judgment on Judah (1:2–2:3), judgment on other nations, and future restoration. God says he will wipe out Judah as he wiped out the world at the flood: "I will sweep away everything from the face of the earth" (1:2). The Judeans have become so idolatrous that God also vows to offer them up like one of their pagan sacrifices. Their only hope is repentance, which *may* save them (2:3). God then pledges to judge other nations as well (2:4–3:8), and the list of deserving nations ends with Jerusalem, which has become as rebellious and profane as the foreigners. The book closes (3:9–20) with the certainty that God will restore a remnant who will honor him.

Significance

Redemption Begins With Judgment

Because Judah will not repent, God must judge. Only the resultant suffering can break the people's pride and rebellion. As painful as that judgment will be, it will pave the way for future restoration, which has become their only hope.

Haggai

Setting

This book records how the post-exilic Jews respond obediently to Haggai's calls to finish rebuilding their temple to symbolize God's renewed presence with them. The prophet delivers four messages from August to December in 520 BC, during the reign of the Persian king Darius I (522–486 BC). The Jews who had returned from Babylon (538 BC) have begun rebuilding, but various obstacles have halted the work. Haggai calls them to resume, and they do, eventually completing the temple in 516 BC.

Summary

Haggai's first two proclamations call the people to resume building (1:2–15) and inspire them once they start (2:1–9). He stresses that they lack resources because they have incorrect priorities, which he illustrates by chastising their focus on their own homes over God's house. Three weeks later they recommence the work, and Haggai encourages them with the promise that although this temple may be less grand than the first, in the long run God will make it even more glorious.

Two months later Haggai gives two more messages to challenge (2:10–19) and exhort (2:20–23) the people in their efforts. He notes that their ritual uncleanness would defile the new temple were it not for God's work to purify them. Also, in order to further encourage the governor, Zerubbabel, Haggai tells him that God values him and has chosen him.

Significance

God Is Present With His People

The Jews who return decades after having been banished from their land need to rebuild the temple because it represents God's presence with them. Completing it reveals they had reordered their priorities, enabling God to bless them.

Jesus changed the way God demonstrates his presence with his people. During his ministry, Jesus was directly and literally God with God's people; after he left, he sent his Spirit to live within us. At the end of the age (Revelation 21), God will again dwell with us directly. Christians today can know that God is with us and will remain with us always.

Zechariah

Setting

Like his contemporary Haggai, Zechariah challenges Jews who have returned from exile to finish rebuilding the temple despite all difficulties (c. 520 BC). The prophet encourages them with assurances of God's blessing and with predictions of a Messiah who will one day rule the world. Though Zechariah's heavy use of disjointed images makes the book challenging to grasp, many of his references to the Messiah appear in the New Testament.

Summary

Zechariah can be split into two sections, the first of which (1–8) addresses hurdles and obstacles the Jews were facing. A warning to heed prophetic messages precedes the record of the prophet's eight visions. The first two include horsemen and horns, signifying the world at peace, then God judging the powers that have harassed his people. In the third, a man with a measuring cord represents God's protection over Jerusalem. The fourth and fifth show God cleansing the high priest (who represents the nation), then a lamp supernaturally supplied with oil (indicating that God will bless the rebuilding of the temple). The sixth and seventh visions picture sin within the community as both a flying scroll and as a woman in a basket being sent away. The final vision repeats the certainty of God's judgment upon the nations. Other messages follow that combine the offices of high priest and king in the same person (which to that point the Jews had not done) and stress right action over rigid ritual. The section closes with promises that God will bless Jerusalem and that one day Gentiles will worship there.

Zechariah's second section (9–14) looks further into the future, with two announcements about an anointed shepherd-king who will be rejected and pierced but ultimately rule from Jerusalem (referring to Jesus in his first and second comings).

Significance

God's Plans May Seem Slow but They Are Certain

Just as by Zechariah's time God had fulfilled his pledges to first exile and then return the Jews to their land, so will he fulfill his promise to send the Messiah, who will shepherd his people and rule all nations. Part of this comes to pass about five hundred years after Zechariah, and part still awaits fulfillment more than two thousand years later.

If God can take centuries and millennia to fulfill the promises he gave through Zechariah, he likewise may take what seems a very long while to carry out his purposes with us. We must be patient and wait for him to act, as he knows the best outcome and the best timing for everything.

Malachi

Setting

In this book the prophet Malachi uses rhetorical questions and answers to challenge his audience's unacceptable attitudes and actions. Malachi addresses issues similar to those faced by Ezra and Nehemiah, suggesting that his ministry is contemporaneous with theirs (c. 430 BC). Eighty years have passed since Haggai and Zechariah promised restoration and glory, and still the community struggles with economic hardship and corruption. Through Malachi, God calls out their errors and assures them that he *will* make everything right.

Summary

Most of the book describes six issues between God and the Jews after the Babylonian exile. They charge that God does not love them (1:2–5), so he points out that, following judgment, he has restored them (unlike Edom—see Obadiah); thus, his past actions reveal his love. Next (1:6–2:9), God rebukes the priests for offering defective sacrifices; his people are to give him their best. Also (2:10–16), the

141

people are unfaithful to their spouses; they must honor the covenant of marriage. Then (2:17–3:5), they weary God with claims that he has been unjust; he promises that he will judge, like a refiner's fire. Further (3:6–12), they have robbed God by withholding tithes and offerings; they are challenged to bring in the whole tithe and see God's blessing. Finally (3:13–4:3), they complain that the wicked prosper; God promises to judge the wicked and bless the righteous—righteousness will be rewarded. The book closes (4:4–6) with a promise that "Elijah" will come to prepare for God's ongoing work (referring to John the Baptist preparing for Jesus' ministry—Matthew 11:13–14).

Significance

God's Work Continues, Though Sometimes "Slowly"

God worked with and for his people throughout the entire time of the Old Testament. Malachi guaranteed that he would continue doing so, like when Jesus came four hundred years later. No matter whether God seems to us to be slow or silent, he continues working for the ultimate good of his people.

Millennia have now passed since Malachi and the New Testament. God continues to work, though not always at the pace we would like. We must faithfully do our part, trusting him to keep his promises and fulfill his purposes just as he always has.

New Testament

Dedication

The Quick-Start Guide to the New Testament is dedicated to the first-year students at Moody Bible Institute who have endured my attempt to teach Survey of the New Testament for over thirty years. I am grateful for their kindness, patience, and encouragement.

Acknowledgments

I wish to thank Dr. Boyd Seevers for the idea to write *The Quick-Start Guide* and for giving me the opportunity to contribute the New Testament portion.

Matthew

Setting

Matthew was in his tax collector's booth when Jesus approached him and said, "Follow me." Matthew immediately got up and followed (9:9).

Matthew was honored. He wanted his friends to meet this man, so he invited Jesus and his disciples for dinner at his house. The Jews loathed those among their countrymen who, like Matthew, earned their living (often in part by cheating other Jews) through the collection of taxes for their overlords, the Romans. When religious leaders known as Pharisees saw that Jesus was in Matthew's home, they complained to his disciples, "Why does your teacher eat with tax collectors and sinners?" When Jesus heard what they'd said, he replied, "It is not the healthy who need a doctor, but the sick. . . . I have not come to call the righteous, but sinners" (9:10–13).

The early church fathers identify Matthew as the author of the first gospel. Some believe he wrote in the AD 60s, others think AD mid-50s. His father, Alphaeus, named him Levi, but Jesus, perhaps to remind the former tax collector that his calling was a gift from the Lord, gave him the name *Matthew,* which means "gift of God."

Summary

Birth and Childhood (1–4)

Matthew opens with the genealogy of Jesus, tracing his lineage back to David and to Abraham in order to present Jesus as Israel's long-awaited Messiah-King and the Savior of the world.

Matthew gives the account of Jesus' miraculous birth from the perspective of Joseph, Jesus' legal but not biological father; Matthew makes this clear by identifying Joseph as simply "the husband of Mary" (1:16). While Joseph and Mary are pledged to be married, Joseph discovers she is pregnant. Assuming she has been unfaithful, he plans to quietly dissolve their relationship, but an angel informs him that Mary has miraculously conceived by the power of the Holy Spirit. Joseph is to name the child *Jesus* (meaning "the LORD saves") because he will "save his people from their sins." The virgin birth fulfills prophecy that God had given Isaiah centuries earlier (Isaiah 7:14).

The account of Jesus' birth and early childhood is filled with danger and drama. Wise men (or "Magi from the east") follow a star all the way to the Holy Land to bring gifts and offer worship to the child. Joseph and his family flee to Egypt to escape Herod the Great's attempt to destroy the true king of the Jews: the order to massacre all male infants under two years of age in the vicinity of Bethlehem. After Herod dies, Joseph brings Mary and Jesus back to Israel; when he realizes that one of Herod's sons, Herod Archelaus, now rules in Judea, he settles the family in the town of Nazareth, in the northern region of Galilee, fulfilling prophecy that Jesus "would be called a Nazarene."

Jesus grows up in Nazareth. Before he begins his own ministry, his predecessor and forerunner, John the Baptist, begins ministering in the wilderness. To prepare the people for the coming of Christ and the kingdom of God, John tells them to repent (turn from their sins to God). He dresses like an Old Testament prophet and is called John the Baptist because he baptizes those who confess their sins. In preparation for what he came to do, Jesus is baptized by John—and tempted by Satan. The Spirit of God descends on him at his baptism, empowering him for ministry; God's voice, from heaven, says, "This is my Son, whom I love; with him I am well pleased" (3:17).

Then the Spirit leads Jesus into the Judean wilderness. After fasting forty days and nights, Jesus is tempted three times by Satan. In his defeat of temptation, he quotes the Old Testament. Then, after the devil departs, angels minister to him.

At this point, Matthew begins an extended account of Jesus' work, primarily in Galilee (4:12–18:35). After John the Baptist is arrested, Jesus begins ministering publicly and calls his first disciples. He teaches in synagogues, preaches about God's kingdom, and heals people of every kind of disease. People flock to him from all over Israel, even from east of the Jordan River.

The Sermon on the Mount (5–7)

When the disciples and a large crowd gather on a hillside in Galilee, Jesus teaches them, opening with what are called the Beatitudes, nine statements of *blessing*—"Blessed are . . ."—which means "approved by God." Jesus promises present and future blessings for a lifestyle driven by God-centered motives.

To make a difference in the world, he says, his followers should be like "salt" (having a purifying effect amid corruption) and "light" (not obscuring their faith but setting a bright example).

To dispel suspicions that he wants to dispense with the Mosaic law, Jesus says that he has come to *fulfill* the Law and the Prophets (i.e., the Old Testament). He teaches that true righteousness supersedes superficial conformity to the Law, and he gives six contrasts between common interpretations of the Law and what the Law intends. He commands his followers to love unconditionally, imitating God's moral perfection.

Righteous acts should be for God and not to impress others. Jesus shows his disciples how to pray (The Lord's Prayer [6:9–15]). He challenges his followers to make becoming godly a first priority and to treat others as they would want to be treated.

He concludes with three illustrations of the one way to enter God's kingdom: the narrow gate (vs. the wide), good fruit (vs. bad), and the house built on the rock (vs. sand). Those who hear him are astonished at the way he teaches.

Ministry in Galilee (8–9)

Along with more teachings are nine miracles, including the healing of a leper, a Roman officer's servant, Peter's mother-in-law, and many demon-possessed and sick as well.

On the Sea of Galilee, Jesus calms a powerful storm and rescues his terrified disciples. Then, landing in the Gadarene region, he casts out several demons from a man.

After he returns to Galilee, two men bring to him a paralyzed friend on a stretcher. The religious leaders are outraged when Jesus tells the man his sins are forgiven. Then, so that they would "know that the Son of Man has authority on earth to forgive sins," he heals the man, who gets up and walks home (9:6–7).

Jesus calls Matthew to become one of his disciples, further agitating the religious leaders when he eats at Matthew's house with those they consider to be outcasts. When asked by John's disciples about why he doesn't fast, Jesus responds with three short parables about the coming of a new age.

He heals a woman who's been ill twelve years, raises a young girl from the dead, and continues ministering in Galilee by healing a blind man, casting out demons, and teaching about the kingdom of God.

Pharisees and Parables (10–13:53)

Matthew identifies the twelve apostles and tells how Jesus sent them out to "the lost sheep of Israel" (10:6). This does not mean Jesus was not concerned about other ethnic groups—in fact, he personally reaches out to Romans, Samaritans, and Greeks. When John the Baptist is in prison, he sends followers to ask Jesus to confirm that he is the Messiah. Jesus tells them to inform John of the miraculous works he is doing, and then he publicly praises John for his devotion.

After two confrontations with the religious leaders over issues related to the Sabbath, the Pharisees meet to plot how to kill Jesus. Thinking that he couldn't possibly heal someone with multiple maladies, they bring to him a blind, demon-possessed man who cannot speak. Jesus heals him with a single command. Yet instead of recognizing that Jesus is the Son of God, the Pharisees charge that he's a servant of Satan. Jesus responds with a warning about "blasphemy against the Holy Spirit," or rejecting Jesus' miracles as evidence that he was empowered by the Spirit of God.

When they want Jesus to show them a miraculous sign, he predicts his resurrection, referring to Jonah's experience of being three days and nights in the belly of a huge fish.

When informed that his mother and brothers are waiting for him, Jesus points out that those who do God's will are his true family.

In this second major message in Matthew, Jesus teaches in parables, simple stories from everyday life that reveal divine truth. When his disciples ask why he does so, he calls the stories "secrets [or mysteries] of the kingdom of heaven" that is, they reveal truths about the kingdom to some while concealing those same truths from others.

The seven parables in chapter 13 are all about the nature of God's kingdom. "The kingdom of heaven" refers not to where believers go after they die, but to a realm in this world where Jesus rules over those who believe in him and live according to his teachings.

Opposition and Prophecy (13:54–16:28)

Even Jesus' own brothers and sisters don't recognize him as God's son. They are baffled by his miracles, for they know him only as a carpenter's son. Jesus' forerunner is also rejected; Herod Antipas, another son of Herod the Great, has John the Baptist beheaded.

Continuing to minister to large crowds, Jesus multiplies five loaves of bread and two small fish into enough to feed five thousand men, plus women and children, and there are baskets of leftovers. This is the only miracle of Jesus that is recorded in all four gospels. Other miracles are not always repeated in each of the four gospels.

Jesus tells his disciples to sail across the Sea of Galilee, and he withdraws to pray; around three in the morning they see him walking on the water and are terrified. He assures them they need not fear, and summons Peter, who steps onto the water and walks briefly before he panics and begins to sink. Jesus takes him by the hand, and as they get into the boat, the wind stops. After seeing his control over nature, they recognize him as "the Son of God" (14:32) and worship him.

As Jesus goes on healing people in Gennesaret, a fertile agricultural area northeast of the Sea of Galilee, he faces growing opposition by the Jewish leaders. He responds to their accusations by calling them hypocrites and warning others about their false piety.

Jesus shows his concern for Gentiles in going to Tyre and Sidon, port cities north of Israel on the Mediterranean. Most Jews avoided these cities because the prophets denounced them (see Isaiah 23; Ezekiel 28); Jesus commends a Canaanite woman for her faith and heals her daughter. After a second miracle of feeding thousands with a few loaves of bread and small fish, he leaves for Magadan, on the northeastern shore of the Sea of Galilee.

Asked again by the Pharisees and Sadducees (a certain wealthy politico-religious sect) for a miraculous sign, Jesus warns his disciples about their deceptiveness.

In Caesarea Philippi, about twenty-five miles north of the Sea of Galilee, he asks, "Who do people say the Son of Man is?" Then to the Twelve, he asks, "Who do you say I am?" When Peter answers, "You are the Messiah, the Son of the living God" (16:13–16), Jesus promises to build his church, and the gates of Hades will not overcome it (vv. 17–18). However, he shocks the disciples when he says he is going to Jerusalem where he will suffer, be killed, and rise on the third day. He uses the analogy of death on a cross to teach about the cost of following him; he also says that some of them will "not taste death before they see the Son of Man coming in his kingdom" (vv. 21–28).

The Transfiguration (17–18)

Six days later Jesus takes Peter, James, and John to a high mountain. There his entire person is transformed in a revelation of his future glory. Moses and Elijah appear and talk with him; God speaks from a bright cloud, commending Jesus as his beloved Son and ordering the disciples to listen to him.

After they descend the mountain, Jesus performs other miracles, and his teaching focuses on the kingdom life that should characterize the lives of all who have truly experienced God's mercy. Though no one is saved by works, anyone who is not being transformed by God's grace betrays a wicked heart.

Final Journey to Jerusalem (19–20)

Leaving Galilee for Jerusalem, Jesus goes to an area east of the Jordan River. He heals the sick and uses teachable moments and parables to emphasize the radical lifestyle that is to characterize his followers, the subjects of God's kingdom. He foretells his suffering and death a third time; going from Jericho to Jerusalem, he heals two blind men.

The Passion Week (21–28:15)

What is known as the Passion Week begins on Sunday with Jesus' "triumphal entry" into Jerusalem and ends seven days later when he is resurrected from the grave.

THE TRIUMPHAL ENTRY, TEMPLE, AND JESUS' AUTHORITY (21–23)

Jesus enters Jerusalem from Bethphage, on the Mount of Olives, about a mile to the east. Unlike Gentile rulers who ride horses of war, Jesus comes in on a humble donkey, in fulfillment of prophecy about Israel's king (Zechariah 9:9). Crowds line his path with branches and cloaks, shouting "blessed is he who comes in the name of the Lord!" (21:9).

Entering the temple, Jesus is outraged with merchants and money changers who have turned it into a bazaar. He drives them out, comparing them to thieves.

Later, on his way back out of the city, Jesus curses a fruitless fig tree and teaches his disciples a lesson on prayer.

Jesus' words and actions consistently elicit anger from the religious elite. They interrogate him about his right to clear out the temple and his claim of divine authority upon his ministry, but he answers with a question they cannot answer. Then he tells three parables that expose their overarching duplicity.

In response, they attempt to trap him with questions about paying taxes, whether there is life after death, and what commandment matters most to God. He responds with phenomenal wisdom, further stumping them with a query about King David's son, and sternly denounces them. Speaking to the crowds and his disciples, he pronounces seven woes on these supposed leaders, calling them hypocrites and blind guides.

Signs of the End of the Age (24–25)

As the disciples leave the temple, they admiringly draw attention to its splendor. Jesus jolts them by predicting its total destruction. Later, they ask him about his return and about the end of the age. Jesus speaks of a coming time of wars, natural disasters, and deception *before* he, the Son of Man, will return—that is, this will *not* signal the end—and talks about a particularly outrageous sacrilege called "the abomination that causes desolation" (24:15). He says his second coming will be visible, glorious, and unexpected, as was the flood in Noah's day. A series of parables stresses the need for believers to be prepared and active in service; he ends with an unforgettable illustration about sheep and goats.

Passover and Prayer; Garden of Gethsemane (26:1–46)

The religious leaders meet in the house of Caiaphas, the high priest, and plot how to arrest Jesus without causing the people to riot.

In Bethany, at Simon the Leper's home, an unnamed woman (probably Mary Magdalene) anoints Jesus with expensive perfume.

On Thursday evening he eats the traditional Passover meal with his disciples. He predicts that Judas will betray him; his death will inaugurate a new covenant that will provide forgiveness for sins.

Then he and the other disciples go to the Mount of Olives. In Gethsemane, he goes off alone to pray, asking his Father to deliver him from the "cup" (26:39) of physical and spiritual suffering, while remaining fully committed to his Father's will. The disciples have fallen asleep, and he wakes them when he sees Judas approaching with armed soldiers.

Arrest, Trial, and Crucifixion (26:47–27:66)

Judas identifies Jesus with the traditional greeting for a rabbi (teacher), kissing him so the soldiers know whom to arrest. Jesus doesn't let his disciples defend him and voluntarily surrenders. The disciples all flee.

The Sanhedrin (the council of elders; supreme religious assembly) wants to execute Jesus, but can't produce enough evidence even though false witnesses testify. Finally, two of these accuse Jesus of saying that he would destroy the temple. Jesus won't defend himself, so Caiaphas says, "I charge you under oath by the living God: Tell us if you are the Messiah, the Son of God" (26:63). He answers indirectly, saying they will see the Son of Man coming from the right hand of God. Caiaphas accuses him of blasphemy; the assembly concurs. They taunt, beat, and spit on Jesus.

Peter, who had followed the arresting party, is waiting in the courtyard. Accused by three different people of being Jesus' disciple, Peter denies it. After the third denial, a rooster crows; Peter, now agonized, remembers that Jesus had told him he would do exactly that.

After sunrise, when the Sanhedrin can legally meet, they officially condemn Jesus and turn him over to Pilate, the Roman governor of Judea, for execution.

Overcome with remorse, Judas tries to return what he's earned for betraying Jesus. When the Sanhedrin refuses, Judas throws the coins at them and goes away to hang himself. They use the money to purchase a field, fulfilling what Jeremiah had prophesied (27:9–10).

Pilate questions the prisoner, but again Jesus refuses to defend himself. Convinced that Jesus is no criminal, Pilate tries releasing him according to a Passover custom. But the religious leaders persuade the people to ask instead for the release of the notorious criminal Barabbas. Pilate succumbs, releases Barabbas, and orders Jesus crucified.

Soldiers mock and brutally beat Jesus. He is so battered and weakened that Simon from Cyrene (in North Africa) is forced to carry the crossbeam to Golgotha ("place of the skull"). Jesus is stripped, nailed to the cross, and lifted up as the wood is anchored in the ground between the crosses of two thieves. The soldiers cast lots for his clothes.

The Romans affix to the cross a wooden placard reading, "THIS IS JESUS, THE KING OF THE JEWS" (v. 37). Some witnesses, including the religious leaders, taunt him, saying, "Save yourself! Come down from the cross, if you are the Son of God!" (v. 40).

From noon until three o'clock the horrific scene is shrouded in heavy darkness. Jesus cries out in Aramaic, "My God, my God, why have you forsaken me?" (v. 46). Bystanders think he is calling for Elijah, and they offer him bitter wine.

After suffering for about six hours, Jesus voluntarily surrenders his spirit. At the same instant the thick curtain that separates the Holy of Holies from the rest of the temple is torn from top to bottom—Jesus has made a way for *anyone* to approach the God of the universe.

The soldiers in charge are terrified. One declares, "Surely he was the Son of God!" (v. 54). A group of women witnessed the crucifixion, including his mother, the mother of his disciples James and John, and Mary Magdalene.

Joseph, a wealthy man from Arimathea, asks Pilate for Jesus' body so he can place him in his personal tomb. The religious leaders, frightened that Jesus' disciples would steal the body and claim he had risen from the dead, plead with Pilate to assign soldiers to guard the tomb. The guards are posted and secure the large stone with a wax seal.

THE RESURRECTION (28:1–20)

While each gospel gives a unique perspective on the resurrection, all four authors note that the women were the first to discover the empty tomb. On Sunday, two of them were startled by a second earthquake. An angel had rolled away the stone that sealed the tomb and was sitting on it. The frightened guards had become "like dead men" (v. 4). The angel instructs the women to tell the disciples Jesus is risen from the dead and will meet them in Galilee.

The women run from the tomb, only to be met by Jesus! They hold his feet in worship. He tells them not to be afraid and then repeats the angel's instructions.

After they recover, the guards enter the city to tell the religious leaders what has happened. They bribe the guards to say that Jesus' disciples stole the body.

The Great Commission (28:16–20)

When Jesus meets the Eleven in Galilee, some worship him, and others doubt, not completely convinced that he has risen from the dead. He commissions them to make disciples everywhere, baptizing them and teaching them what Jesus himself has taught. Jesus promises he will be with believers forever. He is truly Immanuel, "God with us!"

Significance

The Promised King

Jesus made clear that he had come to *fulfill* the Law and the Prophets (5:17), and more than any other gospel writer, Matthew emphasizes that Jesus fulfilled prophecy. More than sixty times he repeats, "This was to fulfill what was written by the prophet."

Matthew's account stresses that Jesus is Israel's Messiah-King, the fulfillment of God's promise that a descendant of King David (1:1) would rule forever (2 Samuel 7:12). Jesus was born during the time of Herod the Great, and the Romans had given him the title "King of the Jews." Paranoid about a threat from the true king, Herod ordered his soldiers to slaughter all boys under the age of two around Bethlehem (2:16).

Like Moses, who ascended Mount Sinai to receive the Law, Jesus went up on a mountain to deliver his first recorded message (5:1–7:29). But unlike Moses, who spoke *for* God, Jesus spoke *as*

God. Instead of "this is what the Lord says," he said, "You have heard that it was said . . . But I tell you . . ." (5:21–47).

And Matthew proclaims Jesus to be even more than the Messiah-King and a new Moses: Jesus is the Son of God, Immanuel, "*God with us*" (1:23).

Relationship, Not Religion

Christianity is about a relationship with God. What Jesus said of righteousness—"Unless your righteousness surpasses that of the Pharisees and the teachers of the law, you will certainly not enter the kingdom of heaven" (5:20)—must have been shocking to his listeners. Meticulous practice of the Law was the only standard they knew; how could they possibly be more righteous than their legalistic leaders? Jesus wasn't demanding more; he was calling for a different standard, another kind of righteousness. Instead of external practice of the Law, which is mostly about relying on one's own efforts and impressing others, his followers are to pursue a God-sourced, love-driven righteousness of the heart.

Mark

Setting

John Mark, who wrote this gospel, had a difficult start to his Christian life.

He was the son of Mary, a widow, and the cousin of Barnabas. He probably was the unnamed young man who shed his garment and fled naked into the night when the Romans attempted to seize him while arresting Jesus (14:51–52).

He later was pleased when Barnabas asked him to go on the first missionary journey. He looked forward to traveling and learning from Paul and Barnabas, two experienced teachers in the church at Antioch. The three went first to Paphos, on the island of Cyprus, but for some reason when they sailed for Perga in Galatia, Mark left the team and returned to Jerusalem. Paul didn't forget or quickly forgive Mark for abandoning them; he adamantly refused to take Mark on the second journey (Acts 15:36–41).

Paul eventually changed his mind about Barnabas's cousin. Near the end of his life, when he was a prisoner in Rome, Paul asked Timothy to bring Mark with him because he was "helpful" in the ministry (2 Timothy 4:11).

Mark was associated with another famous apostle. Peter calls him "my son," an expression indicating that Peter may have introduced Mark to Jesus (1 Peter 5:13).

Summary

John the Baptist and Jesus' Temptation (1:1–13)

Mark's gospel begins with the announcement of "good news": Jesus is the Christ, God's Son. Then a quotation from Isaiah the prophet introduces John the Baptist.

John baptizes and preaches in the wilderness, calling on people to repent for the forgiveness of sins. Dressed like an Old Testament prophet, he announces the coming of the Messiah, who will baptize with the Holy Spirit.

John baptizes Jesus in the Jordan River. When he comes up out of the water, God's Spirit descends on him like a dove, and the Father's voice from heaven declares, "You are my Son, whom I love."

Immediately after his baptism, the Spirit drives Jesus into the wilderness, where he is tempted by Satan. Facing danger from wild animals, he is protected by angels.

Ministry in Galilee (1:14–9:50)

In the first half of his gospel, Mark concentrates on Jesus' ministry in Galilee. Jesus announces the arrival of God's kingdom and demonstrates his divine power over demons and disease. Even the forces of nature submit to him.

Beginnings (1:14–45)

After John is arrested, Jesus announces the arrival of the kingdom and calls on people to repent and believe "the good news."

The first disciples are fishermen. Jesus calls them to leave their nets and follow him.

The first miracle Mark records is in a synagogue in Capernaum. While teaching, Jesus is opposed by an "unclean spirit." Rebuked with a single command, the demon resists yet comes out instantly. Those who hear Jesus' teaching and witness his authority are amazed.

After Jesus goes to the home of the brothers Simon (Peter) and Andrew, he heals Simon's mother-in-law. It is the Sabbath, so he waits until after sunset to heal others and drive out demons.

Early the next morning, as Jesus is praying, the disciples tell him everyone is looking for him. He wants to reach those in nearby villages, so they travel throughout Galilee, with Jesus preaching and casting out demons.

A man with leprosy comes, begging, "If you are willing, you can make me clean." Jesus touches the man, who is healed instantly. He orders him not to tell anyone, but to show himself to the priest as the Law requires. The man "began to talk freely, spreading the news."

FIVE STORIES OF CONFLICT (2:1–3:6)

Teaching at a home in Capernaum, Jesus forgives the sins of a paralyzed man. When the scribes (teachers of the Law) protest, Jesus heals the man as evidence of his divine authority.

After calling Matthew, a tax collector, Jesus goes to his house for dinner. When the scribes and Pharisees criticize him for eating with "sinners," he says those who are sick are the ones who need a doctor. He hasn't come for those who already think they're righteous.

In response to a complaint that his disciples don't fast, Jesus tells a story, in parable form, about old and new wineskins.

The Pharisees charge the disciples with breaking the Law for picking grain on the Sabbath. Jesus defends them by noting that David and his men ate sacred bread when hungry. The religious leaders have it wrong—God established the Sabbath for people, not people for the Sabbath. "The Son of Man is Lord even of the Sabbath" (2:27–28).

The leaders watch Jesus closely to find a reason to condemn him. Knowing "their stubborn hearts" (3:5), he nonetheless heals a man with a crippled hand on the Sabbath. The Pharisees and Herodians begin plotting how to get rid of him.

MINISTERING TO LARGE CROWDS (3:7–4:34)

Jesus' power to heal and cast out demons attracts large crowds from all over Israel and the surrounding areas.

He appoints twelve apostles and sends them out to preach with authority to drive out demons.

His ministry is so extraordinary that his family thinks he's out of his mind. The religious leaders charge that he's possessed by Beelzebub (Satan, the ruler of demons). Jesus says their accusation is absurd and warns them of the "eternal sin" of convoluting God's works with Satan's (3:29).

When informed that his biological family is looking for him, Jesus says that those who believe in him are his spiritual family.

Jesus uses parables, short stories from everyday life, to teach mysteries (new insights) about the kingdom of God. He explains to the Twelve that those who cannot understand them are unwilling to listen to the truth. Some parables are sufficiently challenging that he must explain them to his disciples.

ON THE EASTERN SIDE OF THE SEA OF GALILEE (4:35–5:43)

Jesus' power is so amazing that sometimes even the Twelve are frightened. While crossing the sea they're threatened by an unexpected storm. First terrified by the tempest, they're even more stunned when Jesus calms the raging sea with a single command.

On the other side of the sea, Jesus works three extraordinary miracles. He delivers a man from demon-possession (allowing the spirits to enter a herd of pigs). A woman ill for a dozen years is healed instantly when she merely touches his robe. And Jesus raises from the dead the twelve-year-old daughter of Jarius, a synagogue leader. "He took her by the hand and said to her, '*Talitha koum!*' (which means 'Little girl, I say to you, get up!')" (5:41).

The Death of John, the Works of Jesus (6:1–52)

When Jesus returns to Nazareth, the people in his hometown treat him with contempt; they believe he's merely the son of a carpenter. Because of their unbelief he works only a few miracles.

To reach as many people as possible, Jesus sends out the Twelve in pairs with authority over unclean spirits. They're to travel with a minimum of clothing, and depend on the hospitality of others for their needs. They will challenge people to repent, cast out demons, and heal others after anointing them with oil.

There are three opinions about Jesus. Some think he's John the Baptist, returned from the dead; others, the Old Testament prophet Elijah; others, another of the prophets.

Herod Antipas, who rules in Galilee, thinks Jesus is John, whom he'd ordered beheaded. John had criticized Herod for marrying his brother's wife, Herodias; Herod arrested him. When the daughter of Herodias entertains Herod with an erotic dance, he swears he'll give her anything she asks, up to half his kingdom. At her mother's prompting, she asks for John's head on a platter. Though distressed, Herod consents.

After the disciples return, telling Jesus about their ministry, they try to get alone in a remote area but are followed by large crowds. When Jesus sees the people, he begins teaching them. Then, rather than send the people away so they can eat in their homes, as the Twelve suggest, Jesus feeds thousands from five loaves of bread and two fish.

Immediately afterward, he sends the disciples to Bethsaida, on the sea's northeastern shore; then he dismisses the crowd and goes away to pray. Before the disciples can get safely across, a strong wind stirs up waves that batter the boat. In the middle of the night

Jesus comes to them, walking on the water. He calms their fears, and the strong winds stop when he gets into the boat.

Jesus Visits Gennesaret, Tyre, Sidon, and the Decapolis (6:53–8:21)

In Gennesaret (an area on the sea's northwestern shore), Jesus continues to miraculously heal the sick.

In contrast to the people who come to him for healing, the Pharisees and scribes accuse him and his disciples of ignoring the Law by not ceremonially washing their hands before eating. Jesus calls the religious elite hypocrites, for it's not what goes into a person, but what comes out that defiles him.

Leaving Galilee, Jesus goes north to Tyre and Sidon, Gentile cities located to the northwest on the Mediterranean coast.

A Syrophoenician woman begs Jesus to drive a demon out of her daughter. He tests her faith by initially refusing to help; she persists. Jesus tells her to return home—her daughter has been freed.

Before he heads back south, toward the Decapolis (ten cities, nine of which are east of the Jordan), a group of people bring a man who can't hear or speak; they plead with Jesus to heal him. Putting his fingers into the man's ears, then spitting into his hand, and touching the man's tongue with his own saliva, Jesus looks up to heaven and with a deep sigh says, "*Ephphatha!*" (which means "Be opened!") (7:34). Those who witness the healing are astonished and can't stop talking about it (v. 36).

Still in that Gentile region, Jesus again miraculously multiplies bread and fish to feed more people by the thousands.

Jesus and his disciples then go to Dalmanutha (also Magadan), where immediately he's confronted by Pharisees who demand a miraculous sign. Frustrated by their unbelief, he crosses to the sea's other side. He warns his disciples about the "yeast" of the Pharisees and Herod (8:14–15), but when they don't understand, he rebukes them and reminds them of the two times he miraculously fed thousands of people.

Back in Bethsaida, Jesus heals a blind man.

At Caesarea Philippi, twenty-five miles north, he asks the disciples who the people think—and who they think—he is. Peter answers, "You are the Messiah" (8:29). Then Jesus begins teaching about his suffering and death; this is inconceivable to Peter, so he attempts to stop Jesus' talking about dying. In response, the Lord rebukes him.

Jesus teaches a large crowd about the high cost of discipleship: "Whoever wants to be my disciple must deny themselves and take up their cross and follow me" (v. 34). Any person who gives up his or her own life to follow him will gain eternal life.

THE TRANSFIGURATION AND LESSONS IN HUMILITY (9:1–50)

Six days after Peter's confession, Jesus leads Peter, James, and John up on a high mountain where he is transfigured. His clothes became dazzling white; Moses and Elijah are present, and God speaks to the disciples from a cloud: "This is my Son, whom I love. Listen to him!" (9:7). On the way down, Jesus predicts his resurrection, but the disciples don't realize what he is talking about.

They discover a large crowd arguing with the other disciples. One man complains that they couldn't drive a demon out of his son. Jesus commands the spirit to come out and never reenter the child. When the disciples ask why they couldn't help the boy, Jesus answers that this kind of evil spirit can be overcome only through prayer and fasting.

Jesus foretells his death and resurrection a second time; they still don't understand.

When his disciples bicker over who is "the greatest," Jesus, with a child as an example, says those who serve others are the greatest.

When the disciples grumble that someone they don't know is casting out demons in Jesus' name, he tells them not to interfere. Anyone who serves others in his name is a friend, not an enemy.

Those who cause spiritual harm to others—they're the ones who do damage.

On the Way to Jerusalem (10:1–52)

Jesus, heading south for Judea, crosses the Jordan River (into Perea). When asked by a group of Pharisees if Moses permitted divorce, he clarifies that God has always intended marriage to be a lasting relationship and that people are not to pull apart what he has joined together.

He becomes indignant when the disciples attempt to keep children from approaching him; *they* are heaven's model citizens. He gathers the little ones into his arms and blesses them.

Jesus then shocks a wealthy young ruler who asks, "What must I do to inherit eternal life?" (10:17). He loves the man, who knows all the commandments; it's faith he lacks—in his case, the willingness to sell all his possessions and trust God. When the man leaves in sadness, Jesus explains why it's so difficult for rich people to enter God's kingdom; possessions can be a great hindrance. He assures his disciples that anyone who sacrifices to follow him will be richly rewarded and receive eternal life in the age to come.

For the third time, Jesus prophesies his death and resurrection.

When James and John ask for privileged positions with Jesus in his glory, he reprimands their foolishness. Greatness in God's kingdom is the opposite of greatness in human kingdoms, and those who seek it must follow his example. "Even the Son of Man did not come to be served, but to serve, and to give his life as a ransom for many" (v. 45).

Jesus' last public act before entering Jerusalem is the healing of blind Bartimaeus.

Ministry in Jerusalem (11:1–13:37)

Mark focuses on Jesus' conflict with the religious leaders over his use of divine authority, especially his driving from the temple the merchants and money changers.

TRIUMPHAL ENTRY AND TEMPLE CLEANSING (11–12)

People line the road with their cloaks and palm branches and sing a messianic song as Jesus rides a donkey into Jerusalem. After visiting the temple, he returns to Bethany (two miles east) for the night.

The next morning, entering the city, he curses a barren fig tree, then ejects from the temple complex those who are making the sacrifices for worship into an enterprise of avarice: "My house will be called a house of prayer for all nations. . . . You have made it 'a den of robbers'" (11:17).

Early the next morning the disciples are surprised when they see the withered fig tree. Jesus uses the occasion to teach about the importance of faith and, for prayer to be effective, forgiving others.

Jesus' cleansing of the temple prompts a series of challenges from religious leaders: "By what authority are you doing these things?" He answers with a question: "John's baptism—was it from heaven, or of human origin?" They refuse to answer (vv. 28–33).

Instead of answering them, Jesus tells a parable about tenant farmers who won't pay their rent and even kill the owner's son in the hope of claiming the vineyard for themselves. He warns that the owner will destroy the tenants and give the vineyard to others.

Knowing the parable is about them, they want to kill Jesus but fear the people.

Some Pharisees and Herodians team up and try to trap Jesus in a question about taxes. It doesn't work; Caesar and God are both to receive what is due them.

The Sadducees, who don't believe in resurrection, present Jesus with a hypothetical situation. They're attempting to show the idea absurd; Jesus says they not only don't grasp the nature of the resurrection, they don't even understand the Old Testament.

When a scribe asks about the greatest commandment, Jesus says it's to love God with all you are and to love your neighbor as yourself.

Then he asks the leaders how, if David calls the Messiah "Lord," the Messiah can be David's son. The controversy ends when he warns about their hypocritical showmanship.

While in the court of women, Jesus and his disciples watch people bringing their gifts. In contrast to the large gifts from the rich, Jesus commends a poor widow who puts two small coins into the treasury—she gave everything she had.

The Olivet Discourse (13:1–37)

Leaving the temple, the disciples comment on the magnificence of the buildings. Jesus prophesies the temple's utter destruction: not one of the massive stones would be left on another. Puzzled, they ask when this will happen.

Because they've reached the Mount of Olives, which provides a panoramic view of the temple, Jesus' response is known as the "Olivet Discourse." Many believe his message refers to the Roman devastation of Jerusalem in AD 70, which in turn is a foreshadowing of a period of intense tribulation just before Jesus comes a second time.

Jesus concludes by exhorting believers to be alert and prepared: Only God the Father knows the exact time of his return.

The Betrayal Plot and Preparation for Death (14:1–52)

Mark now contrasts scenes of evil and violence with scenes of love and compassion.

The Sanhedrin meets to plot secretly the arrest and killing of Jesus. Juxtaposed is the story of Mary (14:3–5) anointing Jesus with extremely expensive fragrant oil, which is followed immediately by the chief priests' bribing Judas to betray Jesus.

On the evening before Passover, Jesus eats the traditional meal with the Twelve. Reclining on cushions, he says one of them will betray him. Though he knows Judas is the betrayer, none of the others do. Jesus gives them the bread and the wine and announces that these two elements represent his body and blood. His death will establish a covenant (the new covenant, superseding the law of Moses).

When Jesus predicts that Peter will deny him, Peter says he would die first.

In the garden of Gethsemane Jesus prays in so much distress that he falls to the ground. "Father, everything is possible for you. Take this cup from me. Yet not what I will, but what you will" (14:36). He surrenders himself even though he knows he will suffer brutal torture and an excruciating death.

While he's still praying, Judas arrives with soldiers and identifies Jesus with a kiss. Peter, attempting to defend Jesus, cuts off the ear of the high priest's servant. But Jesus refuses to resist, and when he surrenders, the disciples all take flight.

Trial and Execution (14:52–15:32)

After the arrest, Jesus is questioned initially by Annas, who'd been high priest before the Romans removed him from office. Annas then sends Jesus to Caiaphas, the ruling high priest. Mark gives an extended account of the Sanhedrin's preliminary meeting and then a brief summary of the entire assembly's legal meeting after sunrise.

Peter follows the arresting party but keeps his distance.

The Sanhedrin is determined that Jesus be put to death, but the false testimony of the supposed witnesses is contradictory. Frustrated, the high priest questions Jesus directly. When Jesus says he is the Messiah and that they will see him enthroned in heaven, returning in power, they charge him with blasphemy.

Mark records all three of Peter's denials and also his anguish when he remembers that Jesus had predicted them the night before. After sunrise the Sanhedrin officially condemns Jesus and sends him to Pilate, the Roman governor. Disinterested in religious issues, Pilate still felt it was necessary to question Jesus to appease the Jews. Right away he asks, "Are you the king of the Jews?" (15:2). Jesus tells them they have spoken it. Even though the Jews make all kinds of accusations against him, to Pilate's amazement Jesus refuses to defend himself.

According to Passover custom, Pilate offers to release "the King of the Jews," but the chief priests manipulate the people to ask instead for Barabbas. They shout for Pilate to crucify Jesus.

Jesus is mocked, cruelly beaten, and then crucified between two thieves at Golgotha.

Death, Burial, and Resurrection (15:33–16)

Mark records only one of Jesus' seven last sentences on the cross. At midafternoon darkness covers the land; Jesus cries out in Aramaic, *My God, my God, why have you forsaken me?* (15:34). When he breathes his last, the curtain that separates the Holy of Holies from the rest of the temple rips from top to bottom; the centurion in charge says, "Surely this man was the Son of God!" (15:39).

Mark identifies only the women who witness Jesus' death.

Joseph of Arimathea, a member of the Sanhedrin, asks Pilate for Jesus' body and places him in a rock tomb.

Mary Magadalene and Mary go to the tomb on Sunday to anoint Jesus' body with additional spices; they find the tomb empty. At first they're alarmed, but an angel assures them they have nothing to fear and tells them to inform the disciples "and Peter" (16:7) that Jesus will meet them in Galilee.*

---

*Mark 16:9–20 is not in the oldest Greek manuscripts, but is included in most Bible translations. The passage records additional resurrection appearances of Jesus, the commissioning of the Eleven, and his ascension.

Significance

A Message of Encouragement

During Nero's reign, parts of Rome were destroyed by fire. The emperor blamed Christians and launched a vicious persecution campaign. Mark wrote his gospel to encourage believers as their families, friends, and some of the disciples were being violently murdered. Some were wrapped in the bloody skins of animals and thrown to wild dogs in the arena. (Mark alone notes that when Jesus was tempted in the wilderness he was threatened by wild animals and ministered to by angels [1:12–13].) Others were tied to poles, covered with pitch, and set afire to provide light for drunken orgies. Jesus' warning that "everyone will be salted with fire" (9:49) could relate to the pain inflicted on Christians who were burned to death.

Jesus Is God's Son

Mark makes it undeniably clear that Jesus of Nazareth is truly the Son of God. His gospel abounds with stories of Jesus' power and his authority over all realms, spiritual and natural. Demons submit to his orders; wind and waves answer his commands. The sick are healed, the blind see, and the lame walk. Jesus, God the Son, is worthy of our absolute trust, for all things are under his control.

Mark's gospel is action-packed and fast-paced. Moving quickly from event to event, he presents Jesus as the Christ, come to establish the kingdom of God. These events identify Jesus as King not by defeating the Romans, but by demolishing the dominion of Satan. Though patriotic and law-abiding, Christians need to remember that ultimately we are citizens of God's kingdom.

To exhort persecuted believers to persevere in their faith, Mark emphasizes Jesus' triumph over sin and Satan. He alludes to Old Testament prophecies about the suffering Servant (see Isaiah 53) as the background for his story of the Savior's incredible life. Three times Jesus notes the coming of his own suffering, death, and resurrection (8:31; 9:31; 10:33–34).

The mention of the young man who fled naked into the night is probably intended to emphasize that no one was courageous enough to stay with Jesus when he was arrested. Following Jesus may not always be easy; it might even be dangerous. How will we respond if threatened or slandered or attacked for staying true to him?

Luke

Setting

Luke, a doctor (Colossians 4:14) and a Gentile, wrote the third gospel (likely not long after Matthew and Mark wrote theirs) and the book of Acts. He traveled with Paul on the second and third missionary journeys and accompanied the apostle when he was transferred to Rome as a prisoner.

His gospel was written (or perhaps dedicated) to "most excellent Theophilus." The name means "lover of God," and the title suggests Theophilus was a government official (cf. Acts 24:3; 26:25). Nothing more is known about this man, so it is only speculation that Luke met Theophilus when he was summoned to treat him for some kind of illness.

In his prologue (1:1–4), Luke says his purpose was to assure believers that their faith was based on historical fact, not fiction. He assured Theophilus that he had carefully researched the life of Christ to give an accurate and comprehensive account.

Luke emphasizes Jesus' humanity and compassion. Though he was God's Son, he needed wisdom and power for ministry. Luke records that Jesus was a man of prayer.

Summary

Prologue and the Births of John and Jesus (1:1–2:52)

Luke is the only gospel writer who gives his purpose for writing and identifies the recipient. He introduces his readers to Jesus by giving parallel accounts of the birth announcement, birth, and early childhood of both John the Baptist and Jesus.

The section ends with Jesus in the temple, discussing questions about the Law with the religious teachers. When his parents attempt to reprimand him for not considering their anxiety because they aren't able to find their son, Jesus replies, "Didn't you know that I needed to be in my Father's house?" At age twelve he knew God as his Father.

Baptism and Temptation (3:1–4:13)

Luke sets the stage for Jesus' ministry by describing the ministry of John, forerunner of the Messiah, "a voice of one calling in the wilderness," as predicted by Isaiah the prophet. Calling on crowds, tax collectors, and soldiers to repent, his work anticipates Jesus' ministry to outcasts. Though John preaches the good news, he is imprisoned after publicly impugning Herod Antipas for marrying Herodias, the wife of his brother Herod Philip.

Luke places Jesus' genealogy between his baptism and temptation and traces his ancestry back to Adam. At his baptism, the Spirit descends on Jesus as he prays; the heavenly voice confirms him as God's Son. Luke includes the same three temptations found in Matthew, with the order reversed for the second and third temptations.

Ministry in Galilee (4:14–9:50)

In his account of Jesus' words and works in Galilee, Luke emphasizes that Jesus ministers in the Spirit's power.

Jesus begins his ministry in a synagogue in his hometown of Nazareth. After reading from Isaiah, Jesus claims the Spirit has anointed him to proclaim "good news" to those captivated by sin, particularly the poor and oppressed. His hearers reject his claim because they know him only as Joseph's son; they explode in anger when he reminds them of how God reached out to Gentiles through the prophets Elijah and Elisha.

In Galilee, Jesus demonstrates his divine authority through his teaching and miracles. Luke's emphasis is on his miraculous power. He records thirteen miracles and only one parable. With a single command, Jesus casts out demons; by his touch he heals people of various diseases. He has power even over nature: He calms a storm that threatens to swamp the boat in which he and his disciples are crossing the Sea of Galilee.

Jesus also focuses on training his disciples for ministry. Their training has three significant turning points.

After spending all night in prayer, Jesus designates twelve disciples as apostles. After several months of training, Jesus sends out the Twelve to proclaim the kingdom of God and gives them power and authority to cast out demons and heal the sick.

At first the disciples aren't sure about who he is, but when he asks them, "Who do you say I am?" Peter answers, "God's Messiah" (9:20). Contrary to the expectation that the Messiah would overthrow the Romans, Jesus says his mission is to suffer and die.

Eight days later, Jesus takes Peter, James, and John to a mountain where he is transfigured. While praying, Jesus' face is changed, and his clothes become dazzling white. Moses and Elijah appear, and Jesus speaks to them about his departure (death). A cloud engulfs them, and God announces, "This is my Son . . . listen to him" (v. 35).

Ministry on the Way to Jerusalem (9:51–19:27)

The third main section begins with Jesus' decision to go to Jerusalem. He knows he will die there, but he's determined; he knows he will conquer death and then return to heaven (9:51).

His final journey is indirect, taking him from Judea through Perea to Jerusalem.*

Luke, whose emphasis here is on Jesus' preaching, is the only gospel writer who gives a detailed account of his ministry in Perea. This section, which contains twenty-two parables and just three miracles, highlights two major themes: Jesus' ministry to outsiders and the high cost of discipleship.

Luke 15 contains three classic parables. In response to criticism by the religious leaders for welcoming and befriending "tax collectors and sinners," Jesus tells the stories of the lost sheep, the lost coin, and the prodigal son. All three stress different aspects of God's amazing love for the lost.

The section ends with the story of Jesus and Zacchaeus, a chief (supervisor) tax collector—thus doubly despised by Jews—and the parable of ten minas (coins).

Ministry in Jerusalem (19:28–21:38)

All four gospel writers record Jesus' triumphal entry into Jerusalem as the beginning of the "passion" narrative. Jesus infuriates the religious elite by throwing money changers from the temple. They challenge his authority and try unsuccessfully to trap him with difficult questions.

As in Mark, Jesus commends a poor widow who gives her last two coins to God.

When his disciples proclaim the temple's splendor, Jesus foretells the total wreckage of Jerusalem as well as a time of extreme tribulation prior to his return.

---

*The designation "Perea" itself is not used in the Gospels; the writers refer to this Roman province as "the other side of the Jordan" because it was east of the Jordan River.

Arrest, Trials, Crucifixion, and Resurrection (22:1–24:53)

In the last section, Luke includes events leading to Jesus' arrest, the crucifixion, three accounts of the resurrection, and the ascension. If Theophilus was a government official and might have concerns about Jesus' execution, it would make sense for Luke to emphasize that he was no criminal.

Knowing that Jesus would come to Jerusalem for Passover, the chief priests and scribes scheme to get rid of him but are concerned about the people's reaction if Jesus is arrested publicly. They get their opportunity when Satan motivates Judas to betray Jesus.

While celebrating the Passover meal with his disciples, Jesus resolves a dispute over greatness, predicts Peter's denial, and tells them that in the future they will need to provide for their own needs in ministry.

Jesus is arrested while praying in the garden. Peter timidly follows the arresting party and, when asked if he's one of his disciples, three times denies that he knows Jesus.

In the final phase of Jesus' trials he is condemned by the Sanhedrin and turned over to Pilate for execution. Though Pilate does not think Jesus is guilty, the chief priests insist that Pilate execute him. Jesus was from Galilee—in Herod's jurisdiction—so Pilate sends Jesus to Herod. Herod's soldiers ridicule Jesus, and then Herod sends him back to Pilate.

Pilate tries to release Jesus, but the crowd cries out for Barabbas, a known terrorist. At last Pilate orders Jesus crucified along with two thieves. One of the two mocks Jesus; the other recognizes his innocence. Even the centurion declares Jesus to be "a righteous man." Onlookers beat their breasts, a symbolic gesture of remorse over the terrible injustice of executing Jesus.

Joseph of Arimathea asks Pilate for the body and buries the Lord in his own tomb.

As written in the Scriptures, Jesus cannot be defeated by death. On Sunday the women discover the tomb empty, and the resurrected

Lord appears first to them, later to two men on the road to Emmaus, and then to the Eleven in an upper room.

Luke concludes his gospel with the account of Jesus' ascension to heaven and the return of the disciples to Jerusalem as Jesus commanded.

Significance

Luke, who gives the longest and most comprehensive account of Christ's life, portrays Jesus as "the Son of Man [who] came to seek and to save the lost" (19:10). Jesus came not to conquer the Romans but to suffer and die as the Savior of the world. And afterward he commissioned his followers to take the gospel to the ends of the earth.

Luke highlights Jesus' ministry to the poor, sinners, Samaritans, and Gentiles—those despised and marginalized by most Jews. Jesus is indeed Israel's Messiah, but he is more: He is the Savior of all who believe. After reading Luke's gospel, no one should ever think they have so far distanced themselves from God that they are forgotten. And none of us can look down on another person as unimportant to God. Conversely, Jesus is especially concerned about the poor and the powerless.

God's extravagant love for the lost is plainly seen in Luke's stories of Jesus as the Great Physician. He came for the "sick," those despised as outcasts, not for the "healthy," who believed themselves righteous (5:31). The example of Jesus' loving interactions with tax collectors, immoral women, and the poor compels us to embrace those labeled as undesirable or unwanted (e.g., 7:36–50; 10:38–42; 17:11–19; 19:1–10).

Luke also encourages believers to pray, by noting that Jesus prayed at critical occasions. Jesus was praying at his baptism. He often withdrew from ministry to pray. He prayed all night before choosing the Twelve. When he left the multitudes to pray and was alone with his disciples, he asked, "Who do you say I am?" When he went up on a mountain to pray, he was transformed. After warning Peter that he would be tested by Satan, Jesus assured him he had prayed fervently for him. To prepare himself for the pain of death on the cross and taking on himself the sin of the world, Jesus fell on his face and prayed to his Father.

Finally, we see the Father's heart in a unique way through the parable of the prodigal son (15:11–31). Though the son wasted his inheritance, when he comes home the Father runs out to embrace him. This is a vivid picture of God's unconditional love. Though we may have rebelled against him and perhaps squandered our lives, we can be confident that if we will return to the Father he will welcome us with open arms.

John

Setting

John, known as the beloved disciple or the disciple Jesus loved (e.g., 13:23; 19:26; 20:2; 21:20), wrote the fourth gospel. He was the son of Zebedee, a fisherman, and one of the Twelve. He served Christ as a pastor, theologian, and evangelist.

John states his purpose in 20:30–31: to convince people that Jesus is the Christ ("the anointed one") and the Son of God, and that by believing in him they will have life.

John (1:1–18) identifies Jesus as the preexistent Word (*logos*) who has been with God and is God (1:1). Throughout, John emphasizes his deity; seven times Jesus claims he is the *"I AM"* (God's divine name in the Old Testament; e.g., Exodus 3:14). When the religious leaders question his identity, Jesus says, "I and the Father are one" (10:30). For his claim to equality with God, the Jews attempt to stone him (10:32–33).

For John, wanting people to believe so that they might have life, "life" is both a present and a future reality. The person who believes on Jesus will live; though they die physically, they'll never die spiritually (11:25–27).

Summary

Introduction (Prologue; 1:1–18)

John opens with six amazing statements about Jesus Christ.

First, the Word (Jesus) is actually God and existed even before creation.

Second, God created everything through the Word, who brought light into the world. Though the Word is the Creator, the world he created has rejected him.

Third, Jesus, the Word, has come in the flesh to reveal God's glory.

Fourth, Jesus is greater than John the Baptist because he existed before John, and he brought grace and truth in immeasurable abundance.

Fifth, Jesus is greater than Moses. The law was given through Moses, but grace and truth came through Jesus Christ.

Sixth, "No one has ever seen God, but the one and only Son, who is himself God and is in closest relationship with the Father, has made him known" (1:18).

The Book of Signs (1:19–12:50)

In the first major section, John records seven miracles and seven messages. He refers to Jesus' miracles as "signs," placing more emphasis on the meaning of the events than on their miraculous nature.

Some think John the Baptist might be the Christ ("the anointed one"), the prophet Elijah, or even Moses. John denies he is the Christ and says he's God's messenger who has come to prepare people for the Lord's coming.

After John identifies Jesus: "Look, the Lamb of God, who takes away the sin of the world!" (1:29) Jesus begins recruiting his disciples. They aren't rich and famous, but commoners. But all have anticipated the Messiah's coming and enthusiastically respond to his invitation.

The first miraculous sign John records takes place at a wedding in Cana, of Galilee. When the party runs out of wine, Jesus turns approximately 180 gallons of water into wine. The abundance symbolizes the beginning of the new age of messianic blessing. Arriving in Jerusalem, Jesus goes to the temple and sees the desecration of their holy place of worship. Greedy merchants are treating God's house as a marketplace. He drives them out.

Though Jesus ministers publicly in Jerusalem, John focuses on his meeting with a Pharisee named Nicodemus, whom Jesus surprised by telling him he must experience a spiritual renewal in order to enter God's kingdom.

When Jesus leaves for Galilee, he travels through Samaria, a route most Jews avoid. Jews and Samaritans despise one another; even his disciples are startled when they stop at the village of Sychar. Jesus asks a Samaritan woman for water, then offers her "living water" (4:10) and reveals he is the Messiah both Samaritans and Jews have expected. When she tells the people about him, they conclude that he is indeed the world's Savior.

Jesus returns to Cana, and even though he spends about a year and a half in Galilee, John records only the miraculous healing of an official's son there.

JESUS' MINISTRY IN JERUSALEM (5:1–10:42)

Jesus returns to Jerusalem for a festival (probably the Feast of Tabernacles), and his next miraculous sign initiates a series of conflicts with the Jewish leaders over alleged violations of the Law. At the pool of Bethesda, he healed a man who'd been disabled thirty-eight years. The Jews condemn Jesus for healing the man on the Sabbath.

Jesus responds to their criticism with a major discourse. He claims his miraculous works are in harmony with God, his Father, and appeals to Moses as his witness.

The next sign takes place near the Sea of Galilee (or Tiberias). After Jesus teaches a large multitude, the disciples want to send the people home, but he insists on feeding them. With five loaves of bread and two fish, Jesus provides food for thousands of people with twelve baskets left over.

Only the Twelve witness the fifth sign. When evening comes, Jesus sends them back across the sea. During the night he approaches the boat walking on water. As he gets in they arrive on the other side.

The next day the people are puzzled; they see only one boat and know Jesus hadn't been in it. He uses the occasion for his next major discourse. He says he is "the bread of life" (6:35). Though Moses provided food for the Israelites in the wilderness, the people eventually died. However, if the people eat the bread Jesus offers, they will never die.

When Jesus returns again to Jerusalem, the Jews publicly debate his identity. He amazes his opponents with his teaching. When asked how he knows the Scriptures without any formal training, he says his teacher is the one who sent him—God. This claim further divides the Jews. Some want to kill him; they believe he's demon-possessed. Others disagree and think he might be the Messiah.

The story about the woman caught in adultery is probably authentic but likely not part of John's original account of the life of Christ.

In his fourth discourse, Jesus claims he is "the light of the world" (8:12). When the Jews challenge his testimony, he says they don't believe him because they don't know God and are slaves of sin. When he identifies himself with God, who had appeared to Abraham, they try to stone him for blasphemy.

Jesus' sixth miraculous sign relates to his statement that he is the light of the world. He restores the sight of a man who'd been blind from birth, but because he does it on the Sabbath, the religious leaders are suspicious. They question the blind man, and when he insists Jesus has healed him, they throw him out of the synagogue. Jesus hears what happened and says the Pharisees are spiritually blind.

In his fifth discourse, Jesus criticizes the religious leaders as false shepherds and thieves intent on robbing God's people. In contrast, he is "the good shepherd" (10:10–11), willing to lay down his life for his sheep. As before, his teaching divides the Jews.

When the leaders demand that he prove he is the Messiah, Jesus claims absolute unity with God: "I and the Father are one" (v. 30). Again the Jews attempt to stone him.

Jesus and his disciples leave Jerusalem, crossing the Jordan River into Perea.

RAISING OF LAZARUS (11:1–57)

Jesus doesn't stay long. Receiving word that his friend Lazarus is terminally ill, he returns to Bethany in Judea. Lazarus has died, but Jesus assures the man's sisters, Martha and Mary, that he is "the resurrection and the life" (11:25) and anyone who believes in him will live, even though they die. Then he raises Lazarus from the dead; the seventh and climatic miraculous sign in John's gospel is such convincing evidence of Jesus' being God that Caiaphas and the religious high council scheme to arrest him and execute him for blasphemy.

JESUS ANOINTED AT BETHANY; HIS LAST PUBLIC MESSAGE (12:1–50)

In Bethany, Mary anoints Jesus' feet with her hair, a foreshadowing of his death and burial.

The last miracle has stirred up so much support for Jesus that the chief priests decide to kill Lazarus as well.

When Jesus makes his final entry into Jerusalem, great crowds greet him as their coming king; the throngs do not include the Pharisees. Knowing they are plotting to kill him, Jesus says that God will glorify him through his death.

In his last public message, Jesus talks with Greeks who'd come to Jerusalem for Passover. He has come as the "light" (12:35–36), to save, not to judge, yet those who reject him will be judged in the end, and those who believe will receive eternal life.

The Book of Service (13:1–17:26)

John alone gives a detailed account of Jesus' teaching in the upper room on the eve of Passover. Gathered with his disciples for the meal and assuming the role of a servant, he washes their feet and calls them to follow his example of humility in serving others.

After Jesus predicts that Judas will betray him, he turns his attention to the Eleven. He gives them a new command: to sacrificially love one another as he has loved them. He surprises them by revealing that he's about to leave, but he assures them that this is according to God's plan.

They're anxious; to reassure them, Jesus makes three promises. First, he's leaving to prepare a place for them but will return to take them to be with him. Second, he will send his Spirit—"another advocate" (comforter, or counselor; 14:16) who will be with them forever. He warns that they'll be persecuted, as he has been, yet the Spirit will help them and enable them to witness to the world. Third, he says that he is the true vine, and they are the branches. If they remain connected to him, they will be fruitful just as Jesus had been.

Jesus concludes his ministry there with a prayer (1) that even in death he might glorify his Father, (2) for his disciples' spiritual protection and faithfulness, and (3) for the unity and glory of those who will become believers.

The Book of Sacrifice (18:1–21:25)

The last main section focuses on Jesus' arrest, trials, death, burial, and resurrection. John is clear that Jesus goes to the cross voluntarily. He surrenders to the soldiers sent to arrest him. John records the high priest Annas' questioning of Jesus and then Pilate's decision to send him to his death.

Pilate tries to stay uninvolved; the Jewish leaders insist Jesus is a criminal worthy of death. Pilate offers to release him, but the Jews shout "No, not him! Give us Barabbas!" (18:40). Pilate sets the violent criminal free and sentences Jesus to be crucified.

His cross is between two thieves at Golgotha, "the place of the skull." Before he dies, Jesus commits his mother to the care of John, his beloved disciple. Having accomplished his mission as a sacrifice for the world's sins, he bows his head and gives up his spirit. Soldiers pierce his side to make sure he is dead before removing his body.

Joseph of Arimathea asks Pilate for Jesus' body, and with the help of Nicodemus, places Jesus in his own tomb.

Jesus' death is not the end of the story. On Sunday, Mary Magdalene discovers an empty tomb. When she tells Peter and John, they run to the tomb and also see that it is empty. Thinking that someone has stolen his body, Mary is weeping near the tomb when Jesus appears to her. When she recognizes him: "Rabboni!" ("Teacher"), he instructs her to go and tell his disciples he is alive.

That evening Jesus appears to the disciples, who'd gathered secretly for fear of the Jews. Later Jesus appears to Thomas, who initially doubted Jesus had risen. When Thomas sees him, he cries out, "My Lord, and my God!" (20:28).

The book of John concludes with the appearance of Jesus to his disciples while they fish on the Sea of Galilee. He notes the reinstatement of Peter, the denial of a rumor that John would not die, and a statement about the truth of what he has written.

Significance

More than any other gospel, John emphasizes that Jesus is the Son of God. Even in the first century, skeptics denied that Jesus Christ had come as God in the flesh. Some thought he was a mere man; they claimed the Spirit descended on Jesus at his baptism, but then departed before his death. Others thought Jesus was only a spirit and merely appeared to be human. John dispels both misconceptions, insisting that Jesus has always existed and is the Son of God, in the flesh, come to reveal the Father (1:1, 14, 18).

In John we witness how Jesus crossed social and ethnic boundaries to bring eternal life to the lost. He reached out to a Samaritan woman even though she was looked down upon by Jews and even an outcast in her own village (4:1–26). Even though it was a social taboo to interact with her, Jesus offered her "living water." How do we respond when we encounter people who are different from us? No societal barrier bothers (or is a barrier for) God, and it should never prevent us from offering the water of eternal life.

Jesus is not merely Israel's Messiah. As the Samaritans said of the woman's witness: "We have heard for ourselves . . . this man really is the Savior of the world" (4:42).

In what is called the Upper Room Discourse (Jesus' final message to his disciples before his death), he taught about what they should expect after he left to return to his Father (13–17). Though they were distressed that he was leaving, he assured them it was for their good, and he promised to send another "advocate," God's Holy Spirit (14:16–17). What Jesus said informs us about the Spirit's ministry. The Spirit is a permanent gift from Christ to believers. He comforts, encourages, guides, and empowers believers as witnesses in the world. And the Spirit convicts the world (unbelievers) of sin, the need for righteousness, and judgment (16:8).

Jesus' promise to send the Spirit was fulfilled on the day of Pentecost (Acts 2).

Acts

Setting

Luke, a physician and the only Gentile New Testament writer, wrote Acts. He went with Paul on his second and third missionary journeys and was with the apostle when he was taken to Rome as a prisoner. He uses the first person personal pronoun *we* in several narrative passages (16:10–18; 20:5–15; 21:1–18; 27:1–28:16).

Acts is the second volume in Luke's story of Christianity's origins. The third gospel and the book of Acts were written to the same person, Theophilus (Luke 1:1–4). His gospel tells of Christ's birth and life; Acts tells of the church's birth and growth.

Acts 1:8 gives a summary of the book's geographical divisions. After receiving the gift of the Holy Spirit, the first Christians were witnesses in Jerusalem and Judea, in Samaria, and "to the ends of the earth."

At the beginning, about one hundred twenty believers gathered in Jerusalem for prayer and to wait for the gift of the Spirit (1:15). The book ends with Paul, under house arrest in Rome, courageously teaching about the kingdom of God (28:30–31). Christianity spread from Jerusalem to Rome; the church already had grown from dozens to thousands.

The Spirit was the reason for this remarkable growth. Before his death, Jesus had promised to empower his followers with the gift of the Holy Spirit (John 16:5–7). After his return to heaven, Jesus fulfilled his word at Pentecost. While meeting in an upper room, his followers, both men and women, were suddenly filled with God's Spirit (2:1–4). In the Spirit's power, Christ's followers boldly proclaimed the gospel to Jews, Samaritans, and Gentiles, from Jerusalem to Rome. Each phase in the church's growth took place under the Spirit's direction.

Summary

The Gift of the Holy Spirit; a Replacement Is Found for Judas (1:1–2:47)

Luke dedicates the book to Theophilus and continues the account of what Jesus did after his resurrection and before his ascension.

To overcome any lingering doubts about having been resurrected, he appeared to the apostles multiple times, taught about the kingdom of God, promised the gift of the Spirit, and commissioned the apostles as witnesses.

As Jesus returns to heaven in a cloud, two angels assure his bewildered followers that he is coming back again.

The apostles return to Jerusalem as Jesus ordered. They meet in an upstairs room with several women and the brothers of Jesus for prayer.

Referring to what David predicted in the Psalms, Peter recommends they choose a replacement for Judas, who had committed suicide after betraying Jesus. Using an Old Testament method for determining God's will, they cast lots. The lot falls on Matthias.

On the day of Pentecost, when the believers receive the gift of the Holy Spirit, the now Spirit-filled followers of Jesus begin praising God in tongues (other languages).

This supernatural ability attracts the attention of Jews who had come to Jerusalem from everywhere, and Peter seizes the opportunity. To the assembled crowd, he says the gift of the Spirit is the fulfillment of Joel's prophecy and proclaims Jesus as Messiah and Lord. He gives three proofs: his miracles, his resurrection, and his exaltation.

The listeners are convicted; when they ask what they should do, Peter says if they repent, God will forgive their sins and give them the Spirit. Around three thousand come to faith that very day.

The early church is a close-knit community devoted to the Word of God, prayer, and fellowship. They meet in homes, help one another, and experience supernatural growth.

Miracle and Message (3:1–26)

The events of chapter 3 are somewhat parallel to those in chapter 2. A miraculous event attracts a large crowd, allowing Peter to preach another message about Jesus. As a result, "the number of men who believed grew to about five thousand" (4:4).

While on their way to worship in the temple, Peter and John pass a disabled man begging for money. Peter heals the man, who then runs into the temple. His healing is public, and people quickly gather from all over Jerusalem to find out what has happened.

Seeing the crowd, Peter declares that the man has been healed in the name and by the power of Jesus. He then indicts his countrymen for Christ's death, but notes that God raised him from the dead. He identifies Jesus as the Lord's servant and the author of life. Again he tells them that if they will repent they will be cleansed of their sins, and that Christ will return as the prophets promised.

Growth and Opposition (4:1–9:31)

Here Luke records four problems that threaten the life of the church. The accounts follow a literary pattern of external, internal, external, internal.

First, Peter and John are arrested for teaching that Jesus rose from the dead, but they are released because of the irrefutable evidence that the disabled man was healed in Jesus' name. When they report that the religious authorities have threatened them, the believers turn to the Lord in prayer. He answers with a fresh filling of the Spirit and they continue to preach God's Word.

Second, the early believers are both compassionate and generous, willingly using their resources to help those in need. Luke lists Barnabas as a prime example. In contrast, Ananias and Sapphira are deceitful about offerings promised to the church and could potentially corrupt the assembly. When Peter confronts them, they die on the spot.

Third, the apostles are arrested by envious Sadducees, but then miraculously freed by an angel. When the religious authorities find out what's happened, they order the apostles flogged and command them to never again preach in Jesus' name.

Fourth, the church's growth is threatened by internal discrimination: Hebrew- (Aramaic-) speaking believers were neglecting to give food to Greek-speaking widows. When the latter complain, the church chooses men to oversee equitable distribution.

Luke then focuses on three key individuals who represent the church's witness to the Jews, Samaritans, and Gentiles.

Stephen, arrested and charged with blasphemy, gives a phenomenally powerful defense before the Sanhedrin that so infuriates the authorities they stone him to death. Luke introduces Paul (then *Saul*) by noting that he is a witness to Stephen's execution.

When persecution forces believers from Jerusalem, Philip goes to Samaria. His witness compels many Samaritans to believe, but they don't receive the Spirit until Peter and John arrive from Jerusalem and lay hands on them. When Simon, a Samaritan magician, attempts to buy the Spirit's power, Peter sternly rebukes him. After serving in Samaria, Philip goes to Gaza, where he witnesses to an Ethiopian eunuch and baptizes him.

At this point, Paul (Saul) is not a believer—he's determined to destroy the infant movement. However, he is miraculously converted en route to Damascus when he encounters the resurrected Christ. In Damascus, a believer named Ananias commissions Paul as an apostle to the Gentiles.

Peter and Cornelius (9:32–12:24)

Though Paul had been chosen to serve in this way, God uses Peter to validate a radical and controversial strategy of Jewish Christians ministering to Gentiles.

Enabled to work miracles outside of Jerusalem, Peter heals Aeneas in Lydda, where many believe on Jesus, and raises Dorcas from the dead in Joppa, where many more come to Christ. He shows openness to overlooking traditional customs by staying with Simon, the tanner of animal skins that the Jews consider unclean.

In a vision, Cornelius, a Roman (Gentile) army officer, is instructed to send for Peter. In another vision, God also instructs Peter to meet with Cornelius. As a result of Peter's ministry, Cornelius and his family become the first Gentile converts to Christianity.

When the church in Jerusalem hears about Peter's ministry to a Gentile, they protest, but Peter explains that the Lord directed him and that the Gentiles had received the Spirit exactly as the Jews had, at Pentecost.

Jewish believers scattered by persecution are courageous enough to preach God's Word to Gentiles. Large numbers respond, and the Jerusalem church sends Barnabas to Antioch. After he arrives, he sends for Paul to help minister to the new converts. Believers are first called Christians at Antioch.

Herod Agrippa I, on a rampage of persecution, orders the apostle James arrested and executed. When he realizes the Jews approve, he has Peter arrested and plans to put him to death as well. In response to the church's intense prayer, an angel miraculously releases Peter.

Soon after, when the king accepts being worshiped as a god by the residents of Tyre and Sidon, an angel of the Lord strikes him, and he dies of a painful intestinal disease.

The First Missionary Journey; the Jerusalem Council (12:25–15:35)

Now that the strategy for reaching and teaching non-Jews has been validated by Peter's ministry to Cornelius, the church is ready for its first official outreach to Gentiles.

Under the Spirit's direction, the church at Antioch commissions Paul and Barnabas for the first missionary journey. At first, John Mark accompanies them. They go to Paphos, on Cyprus, then into the region of Galatia (southern Turkey), sharing the good news in Antioch of Pisidia, Iconium, Lystra, and Derbe. On their return trip, they visit the same cities, appoint elders, and encourage the new believers to remain strong in the Lord. Back in Antioch, they report on how God has opened the door for ministry to Gentiles.

Large numbers of Gentiles are entering the church; a group of Jewish traditionalists insists on requiring them to observe the Mosaic law, particularly its requirement for circumcision. Paul and Barnabas, furious at what they see as a distortion of how a person is saved, go to Jerusalem and meet with what is known as the Jerusalem Council. Those assembled discuss the issue and determine that Gentiles are saved by grace and should not be required to submit to the Law. The Council sends a letter to the Gentile churches informing them of this finding.

The Second and Third Missionary Journeys (15:36–21:17)

Paul and Barnabas decide to revisit the churches they'd started on their first journey.

Because John Mark had deserted that team, Paul doesn't want him along. Barnabas disagrees; after a bitter dispute, the two men decide to go their separate ways.

Paul organizes a new team that includes Silas, Timothy, and Luke. They revisit the churches in Galatia and then attempt to go to Asia but are prevented by the Holy Spirit.

They head north to Troas, a port city on the Aegean Sea, and as a result of a vision, cross from Asia to Europe. Despite strong opposition, they win converts in Philippi, Thessalonica, Berea, Athens, and Corinth. Paul and Silas are beaten and imprisoned in Philippi, threatened by a mob in Thessalonica, taught the Scriptures at Berea, and at Athens Paul faces the prejudice of Epicurean and Stoic philosophers. He stays a year and a half in Corinth, where a group of Jews tries to convince its governor that he violated Roman law. Then he stops in Ephesus and Jerusalem before arriving in Antioch.

On his third journey, Paul revisits the churches of Galatia, then heads for Ephesus. Before he arrives, he finds Apollos, an effective and dynamic communicator, teaching about the way of the Lord from the Old Testament. Paul's friends Priscilla and Aquila teach Apollos more fully about the Christian faith and encourage him to go to Achaia.

When Paul reaches Ephesus, he baptizes a group professing to be disciples of John the Baptist and bestows on them the gift of the Holy Spirit.

He ministers in Ephesus for three years, healing the sick and casting out demons. While there, he decides he will go to Jerusalem and then to Rome.

Paul's preaching threatens the sale of images of Artemis (or Diana), so Demetrius, a leader of the guild of silversmiths, ignites a riot. The city mayor restores order and warns the rioters they are in violation of Roman law.

At both Tyre and Caesarea, believers warn Paul about the dangers he would face if he visited Jerusalem. Paul is convinced his journey is God's will and won't be dissuaded. On his way to Jerusalem, Paul meets with the church leaders at Miletus and challenges them to faithfully shepherd God's flock.

Paul Arrested and Bearing Witness (21:18–26:32)

When he arrives in Jerusalem, Paul reports to the church about his ministry to the Gentiles. He is falsely accused of taking Gentiles into the temple's restricted areas, and when the lie spreads throughout Jerusalem, Jews riot. Paul is arrested by the Romans, who think he's attempting to incite a revolt.

Given the chance to defend himself before his countrymen, Paul's speech only inflames matters. When the commander threatens to have Paul flogged, the apostle announces that he is a Roman citizen, which changes everything. The Romans are now obligated to protect him.

To find out why the Jews want Paul dead, the commander brings him to the Jewish high council (Sanhedrin). Paul explains how he'd become a Christian but ignites violence when he proclaims his belief in the resurrection. The Romans rescue him forcibly, and then, to protect him from an assassination plot, transfer him to Caesarea, a man-made Mediterranean port named for Caesar and Judea's provincial capital for Roman rule.

Ananias (the Jewish high priest) and other elders then come to Caesarea and present their case against Paul to Felix, the Roman governor. Though Paul denies the charges and claims the issue is his faith in God through Jesus, Felix declines to render a verdict and keeps Paul in custody for two years.

Eventually Caesar recalls Felix to Rome, and Festus replaces him as Judea's governor. When Festus determines to return Paul to Jerusalem to appease the Jewish leadership, Paul uses his Roman citizenship to appeal for a hearing before Caesar. (The Lord had revealed to him that eventually he would testify in Rome [23:11].)

Before Paul is sent across the Great Sea, he shares his testimony not only with Festus but also with Herod Agrippa II and his sister, Bernice. They all agree he's done nothing wrong; the king even says to the governor, "This man could have been set free if he had not appealed to Caesar" (26:32).

Paul to Rome; Paul in Rome (27:1–28:30)

Luke gives the details of Paul's—and his—passage all the way to Italy. Aristarchus, a believer from Macedonia, accompanies them.

With winter (November/December) approaching, Paul advises the captain to winter in a safe harbor. He refuses, and the ship is fiercely battered. However, as Paul has assured everyone ahead of time, when they are wrecked off Malta, everyone reaches shore safely.

During their three-month stay, Paul heals the sick on the island.

After the group completes the voyage, Paul is not confined to a dungeon in Rome but permitted to stay in a private home, under guard. On two occasions he attempts to convince Jews there that Jesus is the Christ. Some are persuaded, but most refuse to believe.

Acts ends somewhat abruptly, but Luke has achieved his purpose: to tell the story of the church's birth and its growth from Jerusalem to Rome. The book finishes with Paul in Rome proclaiming the good news of God's kingdom.

Significance

Acts tells how God's kingdom advanced through the power of his Spirit. Before he returned to heaven, Jesus promised his followers

197

this gift; when they received the Holy Spirit, they were to witness "in Jerusalem, and in all Judea and Samaria, and to the ends of the earth" (1:8). Then they proclaimed the gospel to Jews, Samaritans, and Gentiles. Within three decades the faith had already spread from Jerusalem to Rome and virtually everywhere in between. None of this was accomplished by human effort; the church is built by the Spirit of God's power. Its mission remains the same today; the zeal and courage of the first believers is an example for Christians everywhere.

Romans

Setting

Paul wrote this letter to the Christians in Rome, from Corinth, on his way to Jerusalem (c. AD 57).

His immediate purpose was to inform the church that he planned to visit them (15:24, 28–29). He had heard of their faith and had been praying for them (1:9–10); he hoped that after visiting Jerusalem he might go to Rome (cf. Acts 19:21).

Paul had a practical reason for this letter's emphasis on doctrine. The Roman church was predominately Gentile, yet there was tension between Jewish and Gentile believers over God's plan of salvation and about lifestyle issues. He emphasizes that both desperately need God's righteousness. God has one plan of salvation: Everyone is saved by faith in Christ's sacrificial death, united with him in his death and resurrection, and indwelt with God's Holy Spirit. No one should boast, for salvation is entirely a work of God's grace, and all those he has saved (justified) he will ultimately glorify.

Summary

The Need for God's Righteousness: All Are Guilty (1:1–3:20)

Paul refers to himself as a slave (servant) of Christ Jesus and an apostle to all nations. He assures the saints at Rome that God loves them, and he greets them with grace and peace. Though he has tried to visit them, he's been prevented by circumstances he does not explain; he is eager to preach the gospel in Rome.

The letter's theme is the righteousness of God—God's action in declaring righteous (justified) those who've put their faith in Jesus. Paul is not ashamed of the gospel—God's power brings salvation to everyone who believes.

Paul first explains why Gentiles need God's righteousness. Divine wrath is being poured out on humankind because they have rejected the truth about God that he has plainly revealed throughout his creation; they've chosen instead to serve dead idols. They've rejected him, and he's allowed them to become victims of their degrading passions.

Then in chapter 2 Paul explains why Jews need God's righteousness. Self-righteously they have condemned others while committing the same sins; they're as guilty as those they've judged. God is just; his judgment is not sullied by favoritism. The mission of God's chosen people has been to bring light to the Gentiles; because of their hypocrisy, the Gentiles have despised the one they've thought of as the God of the Jews. Having a privileged relationship with him and being marked by circumcision as his people, the Jews still violate God's laws. True "circumcision" is not of the flesh but of the heart.

With quotations from the Old Testament, Paul concludes that the whole world is under condemnation. Not one single person who has ever lived is capable of saving himself.

The Provision of God's Righteousness: Faith (3:21–5:21)

From a human perspective, the predicament is hopeless. But the perfectly righteous God is abundantly gracious. He freely justifies (declares guilt-free) all those who place their faith in Jesus Christ, who is the propitiation (atoning sacrifice) for all sins. Salvation is a gift of God's grace; *no one* has saved or will save himself.

In chapter 4 Paul refutes the Jewish misconception that Abraham was saved because he kept the Law. Conversely, as Moses wrote, Abraham "believed the LORD, and he [God] credited it [his faith] to him as righteousness" (Genesis 15:6). David, Israel's greatest king, also testified that God forgives sin apart from works of the Law. As all are saved through faith, Abraham is the spiritual father of all who believe—both Jew and Gentile.

Paul explains in chapter 5 why everyone—even those who lived before the Law was revealed to Moses—is sinful. The entire human race is in solidarity with Adam: He sinned and died, and everyone sins and dies, which shows that all have descended from Adam and have inherited his sinful nature. But that's only the first part of this point. Even though the sin of one man produced the curse through which all inherit innate sinfulness, another "one man," Jesus Christ, triumphed over sin and death. His sacrificial death on the cross paid the just penalty for our sin, and his resurrection from the grave vanquished death to make the way by which, through faith in him, we will *live* forever and without sin. God grants the free gift of righteousness and life to everyone who trusts Jesus as their Savior.

The Practice of God's Righteousness: By the Power of His Indwelling Spirit (6:1–8:39)

Beginning in chapter 6, Paul answers the perplexing question of why people who have been justified (declared in right standing/relationship with God) continue to struggle with sin. He also explains how believers have the ability to overcome the power of sin.

The key is the believer's union with Christ. Using baptism to exemplify this fact, Paul shows that believers have a new status: Joined with Christ in his death, burial, and resurrection, we are dead to sin and are no longer in bondage to unrighteousness. We *have* new life in Christ; released from the chains of sin's power, we are free to serve God.

Paul opens chapter 7 with an illustration from marriage to explain how faith in Jesus frees believers from the Law's demands. Just as a woman is free to remarry if her husband dies, believers united with Christ have died to the Law and so are free to serve God by the power of the Spirit (not by the strength of their efforts). Paul testifies about his personal frustration over what had resulted from his attempts to keep the Law. The Law itself was good, for it revealed sin, yet it had no power to help him overcome his desire to sin. Paul wanted to do what is right; instead, he inevitably did what was wrong. He asks, "Is there no power that can deliver me from my sinful desires?"

He answers his own question in chapter 8: Those who are in Christ are no longer condemned! It's not the effort of trying harder to *be* good and *do* good. Believers have the Spirit, who gives new life and is infinitely more powerful than the sinful nature. As we submit to God's Spirit in our weakness, he becomes our strength. As for the benefits of living in the Spirit, he adopts us into God's family, assuring us that he will complete his work of salvation, help us to pray, and remind us that *nothing* can *ever* separate us from his love.

The Problem of Israel's Unbelief (9:1–11:36)

In chapters 9 through 11, Paul confesses his anguish for his own people, the Jews. The rapidly growing church has more Gentiles than Jews responding to the gospel. This disheartens him. How can God fulfill his promises through his chosen people if so many reject Jesus?

God has sovereignly chosen those whom he will save. His choices are not arbitrary but a mystery we cannot comprehend. In God's plan of salvation he chooses those who respond in faith to the gospel and holds accountable those who reject Christ.

Though many refuse to believe, God will not abandon the Jews. Jews *and* Gentiles are saved when they confess with their mouths and believe in their hearts that Jesus is Lord.

Israel's present unbelief has made it possible for God to save Gentiles. Using the imagery of an olive tree, Paul says "the natural branches" have been broken off and "the unnatural branches" have been grafted in (Jews, Gentiles; 11:17–21). However, in the future, the natural branches will be grafted back into the tree. Jews will see that Gentiles are enjoying God's blessings, and many of them will trust Christ as Savior.

Chapter 11 concludes with a doxology of praise for God's infinite wisdom and knowledge in his plan of salvation.

The Application of God's Righteousness (12:1–16:27)

The final section is about the gospel's practical implications. God expects those he has made righteous (justified) to live differently. The good news not only has the power to save, it likewise has the power to transform (12:1–2).

Because of all God has done for believers, he wants them, in worship, to offer themselves to him as living sacrifices. This means, for instance, using our giftedness to lovingly serve one another (chapter 12), submitting to governing authorities, recognizing that God has established them to maintain law and order (13), and helping believers who need strength to mature in their faith (14).

Paul is confident that the Roman Christians will follow his instructions. He hopes not only to visit them and preach the gospel in Rome but also to possibly go on to Spain. He asks them to continue praying for him and commends them to God's grace.

In conclusion, Paul sends greetings to twenty-seven believers (ten women and seventeen men) and offers a doxology of praise to God the Father and Christ Jesus.

Significance

Romans is the most theological of all the New Testament books. Writing to a church he had not yet visited, Paul focuses on the importance of knowing why and how God saves people who are turned against him and lost without him. Showing that apart from God everyone is without hope, he emphasizes what we can become because of—and only because of—the power of God's astounding graciousness.

1 Corinthians

Setting

Paul wrote 1 Corinthians from Ephesus (16:8) around AD 55, while on his third missionary journey.

He wrote to correct problems reported to him (1:11) and to give counsel to the Corinthian believers concerning their questions (7:1). He addressed a variety of issues, including factions, lawsuits, immorality, abuse of the Lord's Supper, spiritual gifts, and the resurrection.

With a population of approximately 700,000, Corinth was Greece's largest city, capital of the Greek region of Achaia. It was a seaport city, on the narrow strip of land joining the Greek mainland to the southernmost island, the Peloponnesus. Rather than risk shipwreck in the Mediterranean's unpredictable and often lethal waters, many small ships were transported across the isthmus at Corinth, their cargo then reloaded on ships heading east or west.

This setting made Corinth a major commercial center; it was also notorious as a sort of municipal shrine to vice and immorality. The city was famous for its temple of the Greek goddess Aphrodite, located on a mountain, where thousands of priestesses served as "sacred prostitutes." A proverb of the day warned, "Not for every man is the voyage to Corinth," and even nonbelievers knew the moral danger of going to such a place.

The Lord assured Paul that not even a city like this was immune to the gospel (Acts 17:10). Paul ministered there about one and a half years and witnessed the triumph of God's love and grace. However, as yet still swayed by prevailing pagan influences, many of the Corinthian Christians were continuing to live like unbelievers.

Summary

Paul identifies himself as the author, an apostle, and greets the church along with Sosthenes, once the leader of Corinth's synagogue (Acts 18:17) and now a Christian and a co-worker with Paul.

He addresses the Corinthians as saints and reminds them that God has called them and that the Lord Jesus has made them holy. He is thankful for how God has spiritually enriched them, and he assures them that God will present them blameless when Christ returns.

Problems Reported by Members of Chloe's Household (1:10–6:20)

DIVISIONS IN THE CHURCH (1:10–4:21)

The Corinthian church has divided into four factions: people are claiming to be followers of Paul, Apollos, Cephas (Peter), or Christ.

Paul appeals for unity and explains the relationship between the messenger and the gospel message. He contrasts human wisdom with the message of the cross—both Greeks and Jews ridicule it as foolishness, yet the truth is it's the power and wisdom of God for salvation. People aren't saved by a speaker's cleverness but by the power of the message.

Paul hadn't previously come to Corinth in the power of human wisdom but in the wisdom and power of the Spirit. Only those who have God's Spirit can grasp his wonderful plan of salvation; to those who lack the Spirit, the message is foolishness.

By claiming they are followers "of Paul" or "Apollos," the Corinthians are proving their spiritual immaturity. Paul and Apollos are simply God's servants, each with a God-assigned task. He warns about the danger of attempting to build the church on any foundation but Jesus Christ and urges them to become wise from God's perspective.

He cautions against making judgments about another's motives; only the Lord knows a person's heart.

Paul's dedication to the Lord has resulted in hardship and persecution—the world treats him like refuse. Conversely, the Corinthians wrongly have thought they already reign with Christ. Paul is their spiritual father, and when he returns to Corinth, he will confront those who have ridiculed him.

Incest (5:1–13)

Paul is outraged to learn a member of the church is having sexual relations with his "father's wife" (his stepmother). He says even non-Christians do not tolerate this kind of immorality. Even worse, when they should have been ashamed, they are proud.

By his apostolic authority, Paul orders them to remove this man from the church so he will come under Satan's control and hopefully repent. They are to discipline believers who choose to sin. He reprimands them for tolerating sin and notes that he already had warned them about associating with wicked people, whom they are to avoid.

Lawsuits (6:1–11)

In Roman society lawsuits were extremely commonplace, but the believers were ruining the church's testimony to the world by suing each other in civil courts. Paul's instructions are twofold. First, the Corinthians are capable of resolving trivial matters, for one day they will judge matters of eternal importance. Second, they're to settle differences within the church rather than in the courts, even if it means suffering a loss.

PROSTITUTION (6:12–20)

Some of the men in the church have been indulging in sex with temple prostitutes (of the cult of Aphrodite). They see this as simply satisfying the body's natural sexual desires, which to them seems the same as eating when hungry.

Paul clarifies that Christian freedom does not allow believers to do whatever they wish whenever they feel like it. Christians have been united with Christ in both spirit and body; therefore, they are to "flee immorality." Their bodies are now the temple of God's indwelling Spirit; they are to devote this temple to his honor.

Responding to Questions From the Corinthians (7:1–15:58)

Beginning with chapter 7, Paul transitions to answering questions about personal and practical concerns and matters related to public worship.

MARRIAGE AND SINGLENESS (7:1–40)

In Corinth's environment of rampant sexual immorality, Paul encourages men and women to marry, though singleness is certainly an option. Sexual intimacy is a mutual benefit and responsibility reserved for marriage.

In a marriage relationship where one spouse is a believer and the other is not, the believer should not leave the spouse. The influence of a Christian spouse may convince the unbeliever to come to faith in Christ.

Paul lists some advantages of singleness but advises marriage or remarriage (if one's spouse dies) to avoid sexual immorality.

MEAT SACRIFICED TO IDOLS (8:1–11:1)

Paul gives counsel on a question unique to the church in Corinth. Meat that has been sacrificed in pagan temple ritual is then sold at the public markets. For some, eating such meat stirs up memories and passions of their former life; for others, it means nothing—it's just meat. The Corinthians want to know if believers should eat meat that has been sacrificed to idols, especially if doing so offends those of "weak conscience" (8:10–12).

Paul says that though some believers may know that eating meat offered to idols is not worshiping an idol, it is better to avoid eating it if it will negatively affect the spiritual welfare of those with a weaker conscience. Everything must be done out of love, not from superior knowledge.

To illustrate the importance of self-discipline, Paul refers to himself as one who's given up his rights in order to serve others. He has in a sense become a slave to everyone so that he might win some to Christ. Like an athlete, he disciplines himself to win an eternal crown.

In chapter 10 Paul reminds the Corinthians of God's judgment on Israel because they worshiped idols and indulged in sexual immorality after being delivered from Egypt.

He concludes his instruction on eating meat offered to idols with a word of encouragement. He urges them to stand strong, knowing that God will not allow anyone to be tempted beyond what they can resist. They can eat whatever foods they wish and enjoy as long as they do it for God's glory and not to intentionally offend others.

Public Worship: Head Coverings; the Lord's Supper (11:2–34)

Paul addresses two questions related to public worship. Some of the women have abandoned what for them is the cultural practice of covering their heads in public worship. Paul says they should cover their heads while praying or prophesying.

When the church meets to celebrate the Lord's Supper, some are discriminating against the poor, eating and drinking excessively, even becoming drunk. This observance is a tradition passed down from the Lord Jesus Christ for the purpose of remembering his sacrificial death. God will judge anyone who participates without first examining his relationship to the Lord and to other believers.

Spiritual Gifts (12:1–14:40)

In response to the Corinthians' confusion about spiritual gifts, Paul uses the analogy of a human body with its various parts. The Spirit has given gifts to all believers, and all are essential for the ministry of the church.

In what is known as the "love chapter" (13), Paul stresses that without a spirit of love, all the gifts are useless. The virtue of love should be our highest goal.

Although the Corinthians have thought the gift of tongues to be the primary evidence of the Spirit's presence, Paul encourages them to seek gifts that benefit the entire church. Every aspect of the public worship service ought to be for the purpose of spiritually strengthening the church and thus be conducted in an orderly way.

The Resurrection of the Body (15:1–58)

Because some of the Corinthians are rejecting the fact that there will be a future bodily resurrection, Paul begins chapter 15 with a concise summary of the gospel. He points to those (including more than five hundred other witnesses) who saw the resurrected Lord. He assures them that all the apostles proclaim the same gospel, of which the resurrection is foundational.

If Christ had *not* been raised bodily from the dead, then it would be a waste of time to preach the reality of a future resurrection. And if that were the case, the apostles would have no reason to work so hard and put their lives constantly at risk.

Paul explains the nature of the resurrection body with analogies from nature and says believers will need such a body to inherit God's kingdom. He closes with a refrain of praise and exhorts the Corinthians to be faithful to the Lord.

A Gift for the Church in Jerusalem
and Final Instructions (16:1–24)

The church at Corinth also pledged to help the church in Jerusalem, but they aren't sure how to complete their commitment. Paul tells them to follow the same instructions he has given to all churches. They should set aside a sum of money in keeping with their income the first day of every week, saving it for the collective gift to Jerusalem.

He closes by reminding them of his plans to visit and thanking them for their support. He sends greetings from the Asian churches and handwrites a final admonition and blessing.

Significance

As chapter 13 stresses, love is central to Christianity. This is no variable feeling or emotion but a God-sourced love of giving and self-sacrifice. Love is patient and kind. Love "always protects, always trusts, always hopes, always perseveres." *This* love will facilitate a life worth living.

Resurrection is foundational to the Christian faith. If Jesus Christ was not raised from the dead, then we have no hope and are more miserable than anyone. But because he did conquer death, life after death is no fantasy. There is life beyond the grave, and though it is difficult to fathom, our present corruptible bodies will be miraculously changed into new and glorious bodies that will never perish. Accordingly, nothing we ever do for the Lord is a waste of time or effort.

2 Corinthians

Setting

Paul ministered a year and a half in Corinth on his second journey. What happened after he left endangered the church's future and challenged his calling as an apostle.

Though Paul had written 1 Corinthians to correct problems and answer questions, a minority of Jewish legalists still refused to accept his apostolic authority. They charged that he was fickle, dishonest, and incompetent. Here, in the most personal of his epistles, Paul writes to defend himself and his calling. He appeals to the majority to open their hearts to him, as he had to them (7:2), and he moves to expose his opponents as "false apostles" (11:1–15). He explains that his trials and suffering do not disqualify him as an apostle but rather reveal the power of Christ in human weakness (12:9–10).

Titus and another fellow worker carried the letter to the church in Corinth (8:16–24).

Summary

The God of All Comfort; the Ministry of Reconciliation (1:1–7:16)

Paul identifies himself as an apostle and greets the church, then praises God, "the Father of compassion" (v. 3). Though Paul has endured incredible hardship in ministry, he's actually thankful. Through suffering, he has seen even more of God's mercy and kindness, and by learning how to rely on God, he is able to comfort the Corinthians.

In the province of Asia (now western Turkey), Paul faced mortal danger, but in answer to the prayers of the Corinthians, God rescued him.

PAUL'S CHANGE OF PLANS (1:12–2:13)

In response to the charge that he is fickle, Paul explains why he has not returned to Corinth. He assures them that his word is as reliable as the Lord's promises, which have been fulfilled in Christ. He hadn't returned as he'd said he would because he hoped to avoid severely rebuking them, to give them more time to respond to his earlier reprimand.

His previous visit had been painful, so Paul changed his plans a second time and wrote the Corinthians an emotional letter (not included in the biblical canon) expressing his love and urging them to forgive a troublemaker who had insulted both Paul and them.

He'd also needed to go to the province of Macedonia to search for Timothy.

PAUL'S MINISTRY UNDER THE NEW COVENANT (2:14–5:21)

Next, Paul gives a vigorous and detailed defense of his apostolic ministry, including five reasons why his ministry (of the gospel) is superior to that of his accusers:

213

It's triumphant and life-giving (2:14–17).

Unlike the old covenant (the Law; death), the new covenant brings life. Unlike Moses, with a veil covering his face, in Christ the veil is taken away from the believer's heart; he is increasingly being transformed into his glorious image (3:1–17).

Preaching the gospel in a frail human body reveals God's power (4:1–18).

He knows his human body will not last forever, but he likewise knows he one day will have a heavenly body (5:1–10).

His responsibility/privilege is proclaiming the message of reconciliation—how Christ's death enables God to make peace with sinners (5:11–21).

PAUL'S APPEAL FOR RECONCILIATION WITH THE CORINTHIANS (6:1–7:16)

Paul appeals to his opponents to accept God's marvelous gift of salvation and makes an emotional plea for them "to open their hearts" and accept him as God's servant.

It is impossible for believers and unbelievers to serve Christ together. The church is God's holy temple; its members are to cleanse themselves from anything that could defile them.

In a second reconciliation plea, Paul is confident they will "open their hearts" to him.

Returning to the report about his struggles in Macedonia, Paul is greatly encouraged about his reunion with Titus and the report he brought about the church. Though it was initially painful for Paul to send a harsh letter, he is now thankful, for it had produced "godly sorrow" leading to repentance. He's delighted by how they welcomed Titus.

Christian Giving (8:1–9:15)

Paul now turns his attention to the collection of an offering for the Jerusalem church. When he asked the Macedonian churches to help, the Corinthians promised to assist, but for some reason had not yet followed through on their apparently good intentions. What Paul writes here provides the most complete New Testament teaching on Christian giving. He exhorts them to fulfill their pledge sacrificially, proportionately, and joyfully. All giving should be in response to God's indescribable gift—Jesus Christ.

Paul Defends His Ministry (10:1–12:21)

Paul passionately defends his apostolic ministry against false teachers who say he's weak and ineffective and has no right to preach in Corinth. In contrast to the first part of the letter, which was warm and conciliatory, his tone is harsh and confrontational.

Paul claims his authority comes directly from Christ—though he may appear timid, he can be as forceful in person as he is in his letters. His opponents boast by comparing themselves to one another; Paul will judge his ministry not on any human scale but only on his obedience to God's call.

He sternly rejects the charge of having no right to minister there. He'd been the first to share the good news in Corinth, and preaching in other regions also would eliminate questions about his trespassing on someone else's "territory."

It's foolish to brag; however, as the Corinthians were impressed by exaggerated claims from the false teachers, he will "boast" about his experiences. Then, using irony, he contrasts his ministry with theirs. In fact, his opponents are preaching another Jesus. These supposed "super apostles" are not God's servants but Satan's.

After an incredible list of the hardships he's already endured, he describes, in the third person, his experience of being caught up "into the third heaven" (a Jewish reference to God's dwelling place). Then, to keep him humble, the Lord afflicted him with "a thorn in the flesh"; he'd asked three times to have it removed, but it wasn't. Instead, the Lord said, "My grace is sufficient for you" (12:7–9).

He reminds the Corinthians again of his apostolic credentials and asks ironically if he has wronged them in any way. He's gravely concerned about them and so he plans a third visit. He assures them he has no desire to take advantage of them and notes that Titus and his companion also have made no attempt to exploit them.

Final Plea and Blessing (13:1–14)

Paul concludes with a stern warning that he is coming a third time and, if necessary, will use divine power to confront his opponents. He urges them to examine themselves and hopes they accept his correction.

He closes with a word of encouragement and blessing.

Significance

Suffering, in some shape or form, is a part of faith in, or living for, Jesus. Paul says of the troubles he and those with him experienced in Asia that they were so severe they almost despaired of life itself (1:8). But Paul's suffering was not without purpose. Receiving God's compassion, he learned how to comfort others and to rely on the Lord (1:3–11).

Three times he begged God to remove his "thorn in the flesh," and three times God said, "My grace is sufficient. My power is made perfect in weakness" (12:8–9). Through this, Paul learned that in his weakness the Lord was strong. All of us have a "thorn in the flesh" we'd like to be rid of. Our weakness may be our strength, if it helps us to rely on Jesus. Because when we're weak, he is strong.

Galatians

Setting

After the church at Antioch in Syria commissioned Paul and Barnabas for their first journey, the missionaries sailed to Cyprus and then to the Roman province of Galatia (in what is now southern Turkey). They established churches in Antioch of Pisidia, Iconium, Lystra, and Derbe (Acts 13:13–14:28). Then they retraced their route, appointing leaders and strengthening the churches, and returned to Antioch to report how God "had opened a door of faith to the Gentiles" (14:27). They were surprised and encouraged to discover that Gentiles were saved by faith in Christ (without converting to Judaism) for salvation.

But some Jews—known as Judaizers—disagreed that Gentiles could be saved apart from the law of Moses. They apparently went to Galatia, attempted to discredit Paul as an apostle, and claimed that "his gospel" was inadequate. They taught that, for salvation, Gentiles must submit to circumcision and observe other legal requirements.

Paul was furious; he considered this a gross perversion of the good news. He wrote the new believers in the Galatian churches that salvation is—and always has been—based *only* on faith (not faith plus the works of the Law).

Further, once a person has been saved, his true motivation for Christian living is love, not legal observance. As believers in Jesus, they have received God's Spirit, so they're to "walk in the Spirit" and serve Christ in the spirit of love. What ultimately matters is love for God and for one another.

Summary

To refute the Judaizers who were convincing Galatian believers to submit to the Law, Paul argues vociferously for Christian liberty. This defense can divide into three sections: his personal defense (1–2), the doctrinal defense (3–4), and the practical defense (5–6).

Because the Judaizers questioned his creditability, he precedes a typical greeting of grace and peace with a definitive statement about his calling as an apostle.

Personal: "Paul's Gospel" (1:6–2:21)

Paul immediately condemns the Judaizers for distorting the truth and warns of terrible judgment for anyone, even an angel, who proclaims "a different gospel" (1:6).

In a threefold defense of the gospel he preached to the Galatians, first, he had not received his message from any man but by direct revelation from Jesus Christ. He is not self-appointed; God called and appointed him to preach the good news to the Gentiles.

Second, years after his confrontation with Jesus, when beginning his ministry, he'd met with other apostles, including Peter, in Jerusalem, and they approved of his ministry to Gentiles. He had even rebuked Peter for a practical lapse in his understanding of salvation by grace through faith.

Third, it would be absurd to replace faith in Christ with the old legal system. He'd received new life by faith in God's Son, not by keeping the Law; Christ now lived in him.

Doctrinal: Salvation and Faith (3:1–4:31)

By returning to the Law, the Galatians are acting as if they've been bewitched.

Don't they realize that Abraham was saved by faith, and that all who put their faith in Christ are Abraham's spiritual descendants? God promised to make Abraham a blessing to the nations, and he kept that promise through Abraham's *"seed"* (not "seeds"). That is, the divine promise refers to Christ, not to all the future descendants of Abraham.

Anticipating that the Judaizers will question the purpose of the Law if Abraham really was saved by faith, Paul explains that God gave the Law to his people as a *guardian* ("tutor"—one responsible to protect an heir until he is of legal age), to serve until Christ's coming. Because believers are now united with Christ, the Law has served its purpose and is no longer needed. Whether Jew or Gentile, slave or free, male or female—*all* who belong to Christ are now true children of Abraham.

Paul gives two supporting illustrations, one legal and the other scriptural.

First, the Galatians are no longer children, slaves to the Law, but have come of age and are heirs to God's promises in Christ. God has given them the Spirit, enabling them to call him *Father.* Why would they want to give up membership in God's family and again be enslaved to a system that is useless for promoting godly living?

He begs them to follow his example and enjoy freedom in Jesus. He reminds them of the joy they had when they first responded to his preaching of the good news and how they cared for him when he was physically ill. He also warns them that the Judaizers' supposed concern for them is superficial and sinister.

The second illustration is based on a Jewish understanding of the Old Testament. Abraham had two wives and two sons. Hagar symbolizes Mount Sinai and the slavery of the Law. Sarah symbolizes Jerusalem and freedom. The Judaizers are children of Hagar and slavery; in contrast, the Galatians are children of Sarah and are free.

Practical: Called to Live in Freedom (5:1–6:10)

Paul answers the Judaizers' charge that abandoning the Law will lead to unrestrained indulgence of sinful passions. His point is, no one can make himself right with God by circumcision. What God desires is true faith expressed in authentic love.

Believers are free, no longer enslaved to the old life's sinful desires. With the Holy Spirit to guide them, if they follow his lead, they will bear fruit pleasing to God.

Paul encourages believers to help those who fall into sin and to take care not to give in to temptation toward the same sin. He notes the harvest principle: "You reap what you sow." Therefore, they are never to tire of doing what is right.

Final Warning and Benediction (6:11–18)

Paul used an assistant to write most of his letters, even Galatians, but he wrote the closing remarks in his own hand to assure them that the epistle truly was from him.

In contrast to the self-serving Judaizers, Paul's main concern is the preaching of the cross and its power to transform Gentiles and Jews together into the new people of God.

With a blessing, Paul prays for grace, which is far more important than the law.

Significance

The epistle to the Galatians is about freedom. The gospel does not put people in bondage to a rigid set of rules, but sets them free to enjoy life to its fullest. As Paul says, they had been called to live in freedom. Yet we're not to use our freedom to satisfy our old sinful nature; rather, we're to be guided by love and controlled by God's Spirit in us.

Paul insisted that what he had preached to the Galatians is the only "good news." There is no other true gospel. Salvation is through God's grace by faith in Jesus.

The key to a fruitful Christian life isn't stringently following a set of rules, but by faith, allowing the Spirit of Jesus to work through us: "The fruit of the Spirit is love, joy, peace, forbearance, kindness, goodness, faithfulness, gentleness, and self-control" (5:22–24).

Ephesians

Setting

Paul wrote the letter to the church in Ephesus from Rome around AD 60. When he returned to Jerusalem after his third missionary journey, he was accused of starting a riot and was arrested. When the Romans learned he was a Roman citizen, they transferred him to Caesarea and then to Rome after Paul appealed for a hearing before Caesar.

At the end of Acts, Paul is in Rome; approximately two years would pass before his case came to trial. Though he couldn't travel, he continued to teach and write. During this period, he wrote Ephesians as well as Colossians, Philemon, and Philippians. Together these are known as the Prison Epistles, as he wrote them while under house arrest.

Before they believed in Christ, the Ephesians had been immersed in the occult. In Asia Minor (now western Turkey), Ephesus was the religious and commercial center. Pilgrims came from across the Roman Empire to worship at the temple of Artemis (or Diana), one of the ancient world's Seven Wonders. Many would buy and keep silver images of the goddess, believing the idols would bring them good fortune.

Paul had stopped briefly in Ephesus on his second journey (Acts 18:19–21), then was there three years during his third (19:1–20:1). His ministry in Ephesus was effective but controversial. After coming to Christ, the new believers burned books on magic valued at hundreds of thousands of dollars. The silversmiths depended on making and selling images of Artemis; a significant number of people converting to Christianity endangered their business. Demetrius, their leader, organized a protest, which became a violent riot that endangered Paul. He escaped when the city clerk intervened to restore order.

When Paul met with the Ephesian church leaders on his way to Jerusalem at the end of his third missionary journey, he gave an emotional farewell address (20:17–38).

Summary

The epistle splits into two main sections. In chapters 1–3 Paul explains to the Ephesians how, because of their union with Christ, they are his body, already ruling triumphant with him in "the heavenlies." (The term refers not to heaven but to the spiritual realm, where Christ reigns victorious over all demonic powers.) In chapters 4 through 6 he explains how believers are to live ("walk") in the world.

The Position of the Church in the Heavenly Realms (1:1–3:21)

Paul identifies himself as an apostle; he greets the Ephesians as "God's holy people" and "the faithful in Christ Jesus." He extends to them a blessing of grace and peace (1:1–2).

He offers praise to God the Father for blessing believers in the heavenly realms. God chose believers for salvation (redemption) before the world's creation to adopt them into his family. He did

223

this through his Son, Jesus, who by the shedding of his blood freed believers from the slavery of sin and bought the forgiveness of their sins. God did all of this for his own good pleasure! The Father has also graciously given the Holy Spirit to believers as a guarantee that he will give them their promised inheritance.

Paul gives thanks for the Ephesians' faith and prays that they will grow in spiritual wisdom so that they may know more and more about the power of God, who raised Christ from the dead and then seated him in the heavenly realms over all powers and authorities. He wants them to know they have been united with the victorious Christ, who fills everything everywhere.

He describes God's power to save by contrasting their old condition with their new life in Christ. Before, they were natural children of wrath, dead in their sins, but God has made them spiritually alive. They are saved "by grace through faith," not by good works.

God, by his grace, has united Gentiles and Jews in the body of Christ (the church). Though the Gentiles used to be aliens, strangers from Israel (God's covenant people), they've become members of the one body, Christ's. Gentiles and Jews are one new person, God's house, a holy temple where God dwells by his Spirit.

God chose Paul to reveal this amazing "mystery," a plan that long had been hidden but now has been revealed in the body of Christ.

Paul prays that the Ephesians might know and experience the full dimensions of Christ's love, and with praise proclaims glory to God for his infinite power.

The Practice of the Church in the World (4:1–6:20)

Now that the believers know how they've been chosen and blessed, Paul turns to the pragmatic implications. He uses the term *walk* to describe how believers should live here and now, and he exhorts them to walk in unity, holiness, love, light, and wisdom.

Rather than causing trouble, believers are to be united in the Spirit. There is only one body, one Lord, one faith, one baptism, one God "and Father of all, who is over all and through all and in all" (4:6).

After Christ descended (to earth), he ascended (to heaven) and gave gifts to the church. Leaders are to help equip the church for ministry by helping believers to mature in Christ.

The Ephesians must abandon their former lifestyle. Paul uses the image of changing clothes to show how to take off the old life's sinful practices and put on the new life of holiness. Sin—for example, lying, rage, stealing, and foul language—grieves God's Spirit. Instead of being bitter or hateful to others, believers should be tenderhearted.

Every Christian is a child of God; every Christian should imitate God by walking in love. Christ is the supreme example of sacrificial love. Paul lists examples of sins to be avoided; the destiny of the Christian is to inherit God's kingdom!

Their conduct should be consistent with their new life. They used to be in darkness but now live in the light. By walking in the light, they will expose the deeds of darkness.

They should be wise, not foolish. Instead of getting drunk, those who walk in wisdom will be filled with the Spirit.

Paul then applies the Spirit-filled life to specific relationships. Wives should respect their husbands; husbands should love their wives. Children are to obey their parents; fathers should not incite children to anger but gently train them and instruct them in the things of the Lord.

Many of the first Christians were slaves. Paul encourages those who are bound to another to honor Christ in their work, and he demands that slave owners be just and kind.

Because the Ephesians live in a city dominated by the occult, Paul turns from instructions on how believers are to walk (live) to combatting Satan's spiritual forces.

Paul urges believers to *stand* against the devil's schemes by putting on "the armor of God." Using the imagery of a Roman soldier's armor, he lists the instruments the believer dons in preparation for life's spiritual battles.

He urges them to pray and stay alert, and he asks that they remember him in prayer.

Report and Final Greetings (6:21–24)

Tychicus, who brought the letter to Ephesus, will give them a full report about Paul, who closes with a blessing of peace, love, and grace.

Significance

God saved us for "the praise of his glory" (1:14). No one can achieve salvation through self-effort. It's not a matter of our good outweighing the bad; eternal life is a gift from God, which should eliminate any arrogance on our part (2:8–9). We are God's "workmanship," created for good works; as we live out our new life in Christ in the power of his Spirit, we bring glory to God.

The church is the body of Christ, not only a reality on earth but in the entire cosmos (1:22–23). Because we are one body, we should never discriminate against those who are different. We all have the same heavenly Father, the same Savior, and the same Spirit, so we should humbly honor one another and serve together in love (4:1–6).

Philippians

Setting

Around AD 62 the church in Philippi sent a generous monetary gift to Paul, a prisoner in Rome. He'd been arrested in Jerusalem after his third missionary journey, then moved to Caesarea because of a Jewish plot to assassinate him. While there, he claimed his right as a Roman citizen to request a hearing before Caesar. Once in Rome, he was placed under house arrest rather than confined in a jail, until his case came before the emperor.

Epaphroditus, a faithful servant, delivered the gift along with personal greetings from the Philippian saints. In Rome, he became ill and almost died; after recovering, he carried Paul's epistle to Philippi on his return journey. The letter contains Paul's expression of gratitude for their concern and support.

Alexander the Great named Philippi in honor of his father, Philip of Macedon. By 168 BC it was a Roman colony; eventually it was the principal city in the Macedonian province. Situated on the Ignatian Way, linking east and west, Philippi was a center of world travel and commerce. Many Roman soldiers and their families retired there.

The church at Philippi was founded on Paul's second journey. A businesswoman named Lydia, who sold purple cloth, had become a believer after Paul spoke to a group of women at the place of prayer. When he delivered a slave girl (exploited for profit by her owners) from demon possession, she too became a believer. Now unable to use her for fortune-telling, her owners accused Paul and Silas of breaking Roman law. They were arrested, beaten, and jailed without a trial.

While Paul and Silas were praying and singing during the night, an earthquake occurred, breaking open the prison doors. Thinking everyone had escaped, the jailer was about to kill himself, when Paul called out and assured him no one had run off. When the official asked what he needed to do to be saved, Paul said, "Believe in the Lord Jesus Christ." The jailer took them to his house and treated their wounds, and then Paul baptized him and his family.

The city officials (magistrates) found themselves in a difficult situation when they were informed that Paul and Silas were Roman citizens. They dropped the charges, hoping the men would leave town quietly, though Paul called them to account for punishing him and Silas without a trial (Acts 16:11–40).

Paul's letter to the Philippians is perhaps his most joyful epistle. Though a prisoner, he wasn't discouraged; he said, "Rejoice in the Lord always. I will say it again: Rejoice!" (Philippians 4:4). His circumstances actually gave him unique opportunities to proclaim the gospel to the emperor's imperial guard (1:12–20). And Philippians 1:21 might be considered his life verse: "For to me, to live is Christ and to die is gain."

Summary

A Prisoner's Joy (1:1–18)

Paul opens his epistle with a typical Pauline greeting from him and Timothy. (Timothy and Silas were both with Paul when they first ministered in Philippi.) By referencing "God our Father and the Lord Jesus Christ," Paul implies their coequality.

He thanks the Philippians for their partnership in the gospel. They had a special place in his heart, and he prays that they may keep growing in love and knowledge.

Though a prisoner in Rome, Paul does not regret his circumstances; he has taken advantage of his situation to share the gospel. He was able to preach to the imperial guard (1:13) and to Caesar's household (4:22). The former was an elite unit assigned to guard the emperor and political prisoners, somewhat equivalent to Secret Service agents.

Another positive result of his imprisonment is that others have been emboldened to preach Christ. Though the motives of some are corrupt, the apostle does not condemn them; he's thankful that the gospel is proclaimed.

Paul's Philosophy for Life (1:20–30)

Paul's approach is simple: "To live is Christ and to die is gain" (1:21). He is up front as can be about this: He hopes to return to the Philippians, but he also longs to be with Jesus, which Paul said would be even better because then he'd have more of Christ.

The Philippians are Roman citizens, yet Paul encourages them to live as citizens of heaven, even if it means suffering.

Be Humble Like Christ (2:1–11)

Apparently, in the church at Philippi, some of the believers are conceited and self-centered. Paul urges everyone to be humble and considerate of one another, following the example of Christ's humility.

He gives a profound description of Jesus' humiliation and exaltation in what's considered one of the New Testament's key Christological passages. Jesus didn't cling to his rights of deity but willingly surrendered them to become the unique God-man.

Because of his obedience to the point of an agonizing death on a cross, God exalted him. Now, as both man and God, Jesus Christ rules as Lord over heaven and earth.

Shine as Lights (2:12–30)

Paul challenges the Philippians not to "work for" but to "work *out*" their salvation. In a world darkened by sin, believers should shine as stars.

Paul thinks of his life as a drink offering, a supplemental sacrifice to the sacrifice of Christ, and considers it a joy to serve Christ.

He reminds the Philippians of Timothy and Epaphroditus, his co-workers. Both have served sacrificially and with integrity. Epaphroditus almost died from a severe illness, but recovered. Now Paul sends him back to Philippi and urges them to welcome him.

The Privilege of Knowing Christ (3:1–21)

Paul warns about false teachers, whom he compares to ravenous, vicious dogs. False teachers apparently are attempting to force Gentile Christians to submit to circumcision.

He uses a graphic illustration to express to the Philippians how much he values serving Christ. He's proud of his Jewish heritage, yet in comparison to knowing and serving Christ, it's like garbage or dung. Paul doesn't despise his former life, but wants to emphasize the surpassing worth of knowing Christ as Lord and Savior. His great obsession is to know Christ more and more, even through "participation in his sufferings, becoming like him in his death" (3:10). His treasure is the risen Christ's resurrection.

So he chases after Christ, as an athlete runs to win the prize. He knows his reward is not on earth but in heaven, where both he and the Philippians will receive their prize.

He urges them to follow his example and cautions them not to be like "the enemies of Christ," who live only to satisfy their selfish desires and are destined for destruction. The Philippians are citizens of heaven, and one day they will be fully transformed by Christ into his glorious image.

Rejoicing in the Peace of God (4:1–23)

Paul loves the Philippians; he exhorts them to stand firm in the Lord.

To promote peace in the church, he urges Euodia and Syntyche to settle their differences and get along with each other for the sake of the Lord's work.

What is the path to joy and peace? Twice Paul says, "Rejoice in the Lord always." To have peace in all situations, they should pray instead of worrying and focus on positive, wholesome thoughts.

Paul is thankful the Philippians have not forgotten him. They're concerned for him even when they don't have the ability to help.

Through hardship, he has learned the secret to contentment in any situation: it is to trust in Christ, who faithfully empowers believers to do God's will.

Though he hadn't been expecting help, the Philippians sent generous gifts with Epaphroditus. These not only met his needs but also were pleasing to God. He assures them that God, who is superabundantly rich, likewise will meet all their needs.

Paul concludes with a greeting on behalf of other Christians in Rome. "Those who belong to Caesar's household" probably refers to Christians who work for the government rather than immediate members of the emperor's family.

The apostle's last word is that *grace,* God's unmerited favor, be with their spirits.

Significance

The letter to the Philippians emphasizes that a Christ-follower's life should overflow with joy. In any circumstance, Paul had learned to "rejoice." For him, there was no greater joy than knowing Christ and telling others about his Savior. Even as Paul awaited trial and perhaps death at Roman hands, he served Christ boldly and with joy. Like Paul, we can see any circumstance as an opportunity to tell others about our hope in Christ.

In chapter 4 Paul tells us how to experience peace in difficult situations. We're to bring our concerns to the Lord in prayer, focus our thoughts on things that are good, depend on Christ's strength, and trust that God "will meet all [our] needs according to the riches of his glory in Christ Jesus" (4:19).

Like Christ, who voluntarily gave up his privileges of deity to sacrifice himself for us, Paul encourages believers to put others first (2:1–11). This doesn't mean we neglect ourselves, but we should be genuinely concerned about the welfare of others.

Colossians

Setting

Don't touch that! Don't eat that! Keep the Sabbath! Worship angels!
I had a vision! It was all very confusing and, as Paul realized, extremely dangerous. The false teachers at Colossae allegedly had a
different way of controlling sinful desires. Even worse, they claimed
that Jesus is not fully God and that he is incapable of saving anyone.

Colossians, like Ephesians, Philippians, and Philemon, is a
Prison Epistle that Paul wrote while under house arrest in Rome.
He had never been to Colossae; the church there was started by
Epaphras (1:7; 4:12–13), whom Paul had sent to the Lycus Valley
when he was in Ephesus on his third missionary journey.

Colossae, about a hundred miles east of Ephesus, derived its
name from mineral deposits that resembled statues. The area was
famous for the production of luxurious black wool, and though
Colossae had once been economically prosperous, it had been sur-
passed by the neighboring cities of Laodicea and Hierapolis (4:13).

The Colossians had heard the "good news" from Epaphras,
who'd been with Paul in Ephesus. When Epaphras visited Paul in

Rome, he brought tidings of their faith, love, and hope (1:4–5), but also a disturbing report about a heresy that threatened the church.

The nature of this "Colossian heresy" can only be inferred from what Paul wrote in the epistle. It was a "hollow and deceptive philosophy" (2:8) that combined ideas from Greek asceticism, Jewish legalism, and Oriental mysticism. The false teachers claimed Christ is not fully God and faith in him is insufficient for salvation. Paul countered by focusing on the supremacy of Christ in all things, the fullness of his deity, and the total sufficiency of his sacrificial death (2:9–10).

Summary

The Supremacy of Christ (Chapter 1)

Paul includes Timothy in his greeting to the Colossians and tells them how thankful he is for their faith in Christ, love for the saints, and hope reserved in heaven.

He draws their attention to the power of the gospel, the message of truth, the "good news," which they'd received and which was now bearing fruit all over the world.

They'd first heard the good news from Epaphras, whom Paul commends as a faithful servant. In Rome he'd told Paul about their love in the Spirit.

Paul never stops praying for the Colossians. Above all else he wants them filled with the knowledge of God's will so they might live worthy of the Lord. If they live to please God, Paul promises, they'll bear fruit, grow in knowledge, be strengthened with God's glorious power, and be able to give thanks in all circumstances.

He thanks God for their inheritance and reminds them that they've been rescued from Satan's dark kingdom and made heirs with the saints in the kingdom of God's Son. By Christ's death on the cross they have been set free and their sins are forgiven.

Christ is supreme over creation and the church. Among his unique traits, he is the (1) perfect visible image of the invisible God; (2) firstborn (sovereign) over all creation; (3) creator and sustainer of all; (4) head of the body, the church; (5) firstborn among those raised from the dead; (6) fullness of God; (7) and reconciler of all things in heaven and earth.

As reconciler, Christ has made peace with the Colossians, once enemies of God but now spiritually holy, faultless, and blameless.

Paul personifies what he wants for them. A prisoner, yet he rejoices in his sufferings; his afflictions do not add to the benefits of Christ's death, but to the church's growth through the gospel's proclamation.

The inclusion of Gentiles into Christ's body, of equal standing with Jews, is a mystery unforeseen that has now been made known.

Freedom in Christ (Chapter 2)

Paul's labor of love for the Colossians includes the church at Laodicea and other churches in the region. He wants the hearts of all believers united in love and a full understanding of God's mystery—Christ.

Paul condemns the Colossian heresy by contrasting the false teachers' claims with the benefits of faith in Jesus. He tells them not to be deceived by persuasive-sounding false teaching. They must continue to grow in the truths they'd been taught when they first believed.

He warns them not to be taken captive through hollow and deceptive philosophy of human origin and not of Christ, who is fully God. Believers share in God's goodness because they are filled with Christ. The false teachers' core doctrinal error is that they deny that Christ is fully God in a human body. Christ is fully God and truly man.

The false teachers say believers need to undergo circumcision. Paul says believers already have been spiritually circumcised in

Christ and have put off the old life. He uses baptism as an illustration of dying to the old life and being raised to a new one.

And he gives two reasons why following the Law is unnecessary.

First, by his death on the cross Christ abolished all charges of sin against believers, and he triumphed over the evil powers that inspired legalistic demands.

Second, they shouldn't allow anyone to pass judgment on them as to dietary laws and holy days because the Law had been only a shadow of what was to come. Now that they've believed in Christ, who fulfilled the Law, they need no longer follow the shadow.

Not only is legalism wrong, so is mysticism. Those who worship angels and claim to have related "visions" have lost connection with Christ, the head of the church.

Prohibitions like *Don't handle, don't taste, don't touch!* are merely man-made. Such ascetic practices are of no value in restraining sinful desires.

The View From Heaven (Chapter 3)

After refuting the claims of the false teachers, Paul gives positive and practical guidance on how to live as a Christian.

The primary values for the Christian life come from above where believers are already spiritually exalted with Christ, who is seated at the Father's right hand.

Like one changes from dirty clothes to clean ones, believers should put off old-life vices (vv. 5–10) and put on new-life virtues (vv. 12–17). A transformed life is the expectation for every Christian because all are equal in Christ (v. 11).

Heaven's values should guide believers in their family relationships and their work. Paul does not directly condemn slavery but commands those who own slaves to treat them as people, not property, knowing that they themselves have a Master in heaven.

Friends (Chapter 4)

Paul urges the Colossians to pray for themselves and for him, and to be wise and gracious to outsiders.

He reports about Tychicus, a beloved servant; Aristarchus, who is with Paul in Rome; and Epaphras, who continually supports them in prayer.

He greets them on behalf of Luke, the physician, and Demas, and he asks them to greet Nympha and the church that meets in her house.

He instructs them to read this letter to their sister church in Laodicea, and for them to read the letter he'd written to the Laodiceans.

They were to tell Archippus to be diligent in ministry in Colossae.

Paul signs the letter with his own hand.

Significance

In Colossians, Paul describes Christ as the cosmic ruler (1:15–20). He's the visible image of the invisible God; as creator and sustainer of all that exists, he has supremacy over thrones, kingdoms, rulers, and authorities in the spiritual realm. In Christ, all the fullness of God dwells in bodily form. And he is the head of the church, his body.

Paul reminds us of what God has done for us through Christ. He "has rescued us from the dominion of darkness and brought us into the kingdom of the Son he loves, in whom we have redemption, the forgiveness of sins" (1:13–14).

In a sense, we're all born empty vessels. Many try to find meaning through the world's "empty" philosophies. Paul urges us to fill our lives with Christ in whom is all the fullness of God. We do this by trusting him as our Savior, and then by living out heaven's values, putting off the sins of the old life and putting on the attitudes and habits of the new life.

1 Thessalonians

Setting

Paul wrote this letter while in Corinth on his second missionary journey (AD mid-50s).

Thessalonica, the capital of Macedonia, was on the Ignatian Way, a major route connecting east with west in the vast Roman Empire, making it a flourishing trade city. After ministering in Philippi, Paul and his companions traveled this road to Thessalonica. His preaching there led a number of Jews and Gentiles to believe in Jesus (Acts 17:4).

But he also faced opposition. When the new believers were charged with rebellion against Caesar (Acts 17:5–8), Paul departed prematurely and traveled on to Berea, Athens, and Corinth. He tried to return more than once but was blocked by circumstances he attributed to Satan (1 Thessalonians 2:18). His concern for this new church prompted him to send his co-worker Timothy to find out about their welfare and to "strengthen and encourage" them in their faith (3:1–2).

Timothy returned with an encouraging report: Although the church was experiencing persecution and needed to grow more in their faith, they'd become a model church (3:7–8). From Corinth, Paul wrote to encourage them to keep growing in faith, love, and hope despite persecution. About six months after writing 1 Thessalonians, he wrote 2 Thessalonians to refute erroneous teaching about the day of the Lord (2:2).

Summary

Personal Insight (1:1–3:13)

Paul greets the believers and gives thanks to God because they've grown in their work of faith, their labor of love, and their steadfast hope in Jesus.

He commends the church, defends his ministry, and encourages them to remain strong in their faith.

A MODEL CHURCH (1:4–10)

Paul is certain God had chosen them because of their enthusiastic response to the good news. They had received Paul's message with power and joy from the Holy Spirit.

They are a model church. Everyone throughout the neighboring Macedonian cities knows how they had turned from idols to serve the living and true God. Paul assures them they will be delivered from "the coming wrath" (v. 10).

He ends his commendation with a reference to Christ's return, which he mentions in every chapter (1:10; 2:19; 3:13; 4:13–18; 5:23).

A MINISTRY OF INTEGRITY (2:1–3:13)

Paul defends his motives and ministry from when he'd visited them. Though he'd suffered at Philippi, God had given him the courage to preach at Thessalonica. Unlike some itinerant teachers, he is honest, truly interested in serving God and not getting rich by deceitful means.

He uses two insightful illustrations to describe his love for them. He cares for them like a nursing mother and instructs them like a father.

He challenges them to live worthy of their calling to share in God's kingdom.

He's exceedingly thankful for their response to the good news. They received his words as the Word of God.

He assures them they're not alone in their suffering and that God's wrath will come on their persecutors.

Paul is deeply concerned for their church. He'd been torn away from them and then also somehow prevented by Satan from returning.

He's greatly encouraged by Timothy's report about their faith and love, and that they want to see Paul as much as he wants to see them. He can't thank God enough for their steadfast faith.

He hopes to see them soon and prays for their growth in love and holiness.

Practical Instructions (4:1–5:22)

Paul gives guidance about daily Christian living, death, and the day of the Lord.

He challenges them to live to please God, especially in the area of sexual morality. It is God's will that they control their sexual passions.

Though they are a loving church, he urges them to love one another even more.

As believers, they're to be model citizens by earning their own living.

Because of their concern for what will happen to those who had already died before Christ returns, he assures them both the living and the dead will meet the Lord in the air.

He guarantees they won't be surprised on the day he does return. They are "children of the light," not of "darkness" (5:5).

Paul closes with his expectations for them, primarily about relationships with other believers.

To live actively and usefully, they must hold fast to what is good and abstain from every form of evil.

Prayer and Blessing (5:23–28)

Paul prays that the God of peace will make them holy in every way. He asks them to pray for him and his co-workers, and to greet everyone.

He blesses them with grace.

Significance

The remarkable conversion of the Thessalonians was a testimony to the living God. Like them, when we are transformed by the Spirit's power, we become living witnesses to the power of faith, love, and hope in Christ Jesus (1:2–10).

We will all face the bitterness of physical death. These words of Paul should inspire us with hope: "We do not want you to be uninformed about those who sleep in death, so that you do not grieve like the rest of mankind, who have no hope. For we believe that Jesus died and rose again, and so we believe that God will bring with Jesus those who have fallen asleep in him" (4:13–14).

2 Thessalonians

Setting

Paul wrote 2 Thessalonians (AD mid-50s) about six months after the first letter.

After he'd preached the good news of Jesus, persecution forced him to leave. After arriving in Corinth, he was concerned about the church and sent Timothy back to Thessalonica. He wrote 1 Thessalonians in response to Timothy's encouraging report.

Later he heard that the Thessalonians had received a confusing letter, supposedly from him, informing them that "the day of Lord" had already come. This was false, and the apostle wrote his second letter to correct their understanding. He also encouraged them to remain faithful to Christ, and he reprimanded some who were lazy and not working to earn a living.

Summary

Comfort (1:1–12)

Paul greets the church at Thessalonica, wishing them grace and peace in the name of God the Father and the Lord Jesus Christ.

He's thankful for their perseverance. In the face of persecution and painful hardships, they are continuing to grow in faith and love.

Intense suffering, though, has raised a question about God's justice. Paul guarantees that God is just and explains that their suffering is evidence that they are worthy of the kingdom. He assures them they'll be rescued when Christ returns in blazing fire, judging and punishing those who refuse to believe. On that same day, Jesus will be glorified in those who believe in him.

Paul prays that they will remain worthy of their calling and bring honor to Christ's name. The motivation for his request is God's power and grace.

Correction (2:1–17)

Paul addresses the false teaching in another letter alleged to have come from him.

He is adamant. They should not be alarmed; they have not missed the day of the Lord. Prior to that day, there will be a rebellion followed by the revealing of "the lawless one." This man will exalt himself, even claiming he is God.

The Thessalonians need to remember that "the day of the Lord will not come until the rebellion occurs and the man of lawlessness is revealed" (2:3). He [Antichrist] is held back, "so that he may be revealed at the proper time" (v. 6). When that happens, Christ will destroy him by "the splendor of his coming" (v. 8).

"The lawless one" is an agent of Satan who will possess power to deceive. Many will believe his lies, but Paul wants the Thessalonians to know they are loved by God and saved by his grace. They should hold firmly to what they have been taught.

Commands (3:1–15)

Paul asks them to pray for him and his companions. He is confident they will obey his instructions and anticipates that God will fill their hearts with love.

Because some had stopped working and become busybodies, Paul gave this command: "The one who is unwilling to work shall not eat" (3:10).

He encourages those who were working not to grow weary in doing good and to avoid those who are disobedient to his instructions.

A Benediction of Peace (3:16–18)

Paul prays that the Lord of peace will give them peace at all times in every way. He signs his own greeting and commends them to the grace of the Lord Jesus Christ.

Significance

Believers in Thessalonica were persevering, even though persecuted. Their suffering, however, caused them to question God's justice. Hard times can do that. When we experience unexpected and seemingly undeserved hardship, we wonder why. Paul's words of encouragement assure us that God is just. We are to press on in all circumstances, knowing that God ultimately will balance the scales of justice. We will be glorified with Christ, and those who have rejected him will be punished.

1 Timothy

Setting

Paul wrote all three Pastoral Epistles—1 Timothy, 2 Timothy, and Titus—between AD 62 or 63 and AD 67. These are addressed to individuals rather than churches, and they're called pastoral because they instruct Timothy and Titus, Paul's pastoral assistants, on matters related to the church's organization and function.

After his release from house arrest (Acts 28:30–31), the apostle continued to minister in the Mediterranean area. He assigned Timothy to the Ephesus church (1 Timothy 1:3–4) and Titus to the church in Crete (Titus 1:4–5). Both men faced the challenges of organizing the church, teaching the Christian way of life, and refuting false teaching.

The expression "this is a trustworthy statement," occurs numerous times in these three letters, but not in any other epistles. Paul may have used it to emphasize key teaching points, or it may refer to truths that the early church had determined were foundational to the Christian faith.

After about two more years, during Nero's rule, Paul was arrested a second time and held in Rome's harsh Mamertine Prison. He asked Timothy to bring his cloak and his scrolls (2 Timothy

4:13) because he was confined to an underground cell (19 × 10 × 6.5 feet), with only a ceiling hole for access. Knowing he'd likely be killed, he wrote 2 Timothy, his last letter to exhort the young man to faithfully pass on to others what he'd taught him (2:1–2).

According to tradition, Paul, as a Roman citizen, was executed by beheading rather than crucifixion in about AD 67.

Summary

Make the Most of Your Time (1:1–20)

Paul identifies himself as an apostle, greets Timothy, and adds mercy to his standard greeting of grace and peace.

He begins by charging Timothy to silence false teachers who are misusing the Law. Rather than speculate on useless "myths and endless genealogies" (v. 4), Timothy has the opportunity to refute false doctrines and encourage righteous living.

Paul refers to his own conversion experience as an example of how faith in Christ Jesus can transform even the worst of sinners (as he considers himself to have been).

He charges Timothy to defend the faith and informs him about two men Paul had put out of the church because of their heretical teaching.

On Roles and Responsibilities (2:1–15)

Because the false teachers had misinformed the church about crucial aspects of the ministry, Paul gives instructions on prayer, the conduct of women, and the qualifications for elders and deacons.

He urges believers to pray for the salvation of all, and he reminds the church that there's only "one God and one mediator between God and mankind," Christ Jesus (vv. 1–5).

He wants men to pray. He wants women to dress modestly, with decency and propriety.

Because of the threat to the structure of the family and loss of gender distinctions in the church at Ephesus, Paul corrects misunderstandings about creation and the fall. He encourages women there to learn without asserting themselves in positions of authority, recognizing that they have an important function in marriage.

Qualifications for Elders and Deacons (3:1–13)

Paul identifies two leadership roles in the church. He encourages men to seek to serve as elders, though they must be qualified to do so, and lists the character-focused qualifications for both elders and deacons.

The Church and the Mystery of Christ (3:14–16)

These verses are the center of the epistle and explain why Paul is concerned about the threat from false teachers. The church is not merely a group that meets together for social or civic activities. The early churches usually met in homes; he describes the church as a God-indwelt household that is responsible for upholding the truth.

From what may have been a hymn of the early church (v. 16), Paul explains why Christ came into the world. Jesus was vindicated by the Spirit, seen by angels, preached among the nations, believed on in the world, and taken up in glory.

Instructions to Timothy (4:1–16)

Timothy should not be alarmed by the coming of false teachers. The Holy Spirit warned about the coming of men inspired by demons; they would be hypocrites and liars.

In contrast, Timothy should serve with integrity and train himself to be godly. Though young, he need not be intimidated; he should remember why the elders commissioned him, set an example of how to live, and faithfully teach the Scriptures.

Instructions to Various Groups (5:1–6:2a)

By the time Paul wrote these epistles, the church had developed an organizational structure; various groups within the congregation could be identified. He gives guidance concerning older and younger men and women, widows, elders, and slaves.

The church should equally respect both men and women, and men should particularly respect the purity of younger women.

The ancient world had no welfare programs. Without family members to help, widows would struggle to survive. Paul says the church should take care of those who truly need help. If a widow has family members who can care for her, the church is not responsible. Older widows should devote themselves to serving others; younger widows should consider remarriage.

On the church's responsibility to elders, Paul quotes Deuteronomy 25:4 as the basis for paying those who preach and teach. False teachers made unsubstantiated charges against some elders; Paul says accusations must be confirmed by two or three witnesses. If a leader sins publicly, he should be publicly rebuked as a warning to others.

He advises Timothy not to drink only water but also to take some wine for a kind of stomach ailment and other illnesses.

Slaves should respect their owners and work hard as a testimony of their faith in God. If their owners are believers, all the more reason to show respect.

What Timothy Should Teach (6:2b–21)

The false teachers are arrogant and divisive; Timothy, conversely, is to teach truth that promotes a godly life, brings contentment, and avoids the peril of loving money.

Again Paul urges him to vigorously pursue a godly life and not to do anything that might arouse suspicion about his integrity. The reason for diligence in these matters is the certainty of the Lord Jesus Christ's glorious return.

Those who are rich are to help others, storing up treasure in heaven, not on earth.

Paul concludes with a final charge for Timothy to avoid foolish discussions and then commends him to God's grace.

Significance

Pastoring a church can be difficult even if you aren't young. In Ephesus, Timothy faced a daunting challenge. He was inexperienced; the church was threatened by false teachers. Paul urged him to "fight the battle well" (1:18), which meant he must safeguard sound doctrine, appoint and instruct mature leaders, watch closely his personal life, and tactfully correct and instruct various groups in the church. Paul's counsel is valuable advice for pastors today.

Timothy ministered under the shadow of the temple of Artemis, one of Seven Wonders of the ancient world. Yet Paul said it is the church that is "the pillar and foundation of the truth" (3:15). God is the source of truth, and the church is responsible to put the truth on display for the world to see.

"Train yourself to be godly" is an athletic metaphor with which Paul urged Timothy to discipline himself for spiritual fitness (4:7). An active lifestyle is a healthy one, and while Paul didn't at all disparage exercise, he emphasized the importance of the spiritual disciplines. Training for godliness brings blessing in this life and in the life to come (4:8).

Paul also did not condemn wealth, but he warned about "the love of money" (6:10). The relentless drive to acquire can plunge a person into ruin and destruction. And we can't buy contentment. Better to pursue godliness and be content with what God provides. Trust in God; help those in need. Generosity is an eternal investment (6:17–19).

2 Timothy

Setting

Paul wrote 2 Timothy from a prison cell in Rome about AD 64–65. After his first imprisonment, Paul had been freed and went on serving for about two years. He'd sent Timothy to Ephesus, Titus to Crete. Both encountered false teachers who distorted what Paul taught and advocated immoral lifestyles. Paul wrote 1 Timothy and Titus to instruct and encourage them. After being re-incarcerated, this time in the Mamertine Prison, he realized his life and ministry were coming to an end. Paul wrote 2 Timothy to emphasize the need to pass the Christian faith from generation to generation (2:1–2) and to request that Timothy come to Rome as soon as possible (3:21).

Summary

Don't Be Ashamed (1:1–18)

Paul identifies himself as an apostle and greets Timothy. He's older now than when they met and is especially thankful for his young son in the faith. He prays for him, remembers their emotional parting, and hopes to see him soon.

He reminds Timothy of his Christian heritage, his gift for ministry, and how Paul had ordained him for ministry. Timothy should work to overcome his timidity and be strong in the Lord; in coming to Rome and continuing in ministry, he must be prepared to suffer. To strengthen his resolve for a holy life, Paul reminds him that God saved him through the grace of Christ Jesus.

Paul, imprisoned and likely soon to be executed, is not ashamed; he's absolutely certain that the "deposit" he has entrusted to God is safe. He urges Timothy to faithfully guard the truth he had received from Paul.

He uses a negative example of some who deserted him and praised the positive example of Onesiphorus and his household.

The Grace of God and the Example of Christ (2:1–13)

Paul knows Timothy will face the same kind of hardships he's experienced in serving Christ. He uses four word pictures to urge Timothy "to be strong in the grace that is in Christ Jesus": a teacher, a soldier, an athlete, and a farmer.

He refers to Christ's example, suffering yet victorious even over death. Preaching the good news is why Paul has been imprisoned. But even though he is in chains, the word of God is not chained. He's willing to endure anything for the salvation of others.

The "trustworthy saying" in verses 11–13 emphasizes God's faithfulness.

Become a Pure Vessel and a Gentle Teacher (2:14–26)

Paul adamantly commands Timothy to stop the false teachers from disrupting the church with useless and destructive arguments. Instead, he should do his best to teach the truth, avoiding the contagious heresy taught by men like Hymenaeus and Philetus.

It is absolutely essential that believers turn away from evil. Using an analogy from a household where there are vessels of gold and silver and also wood and clay, Paul instructs Timothy to keep himself pure, useful for every good work.

As the Lord's servant, he must not get involved in bitter and divisive arguments, but should patiently and gently instruct others, even those who have rejected the truth.

The Last Days (3:1–9)

Paul tells Timothy what to expect if indeed they are living in the last days. People will be unimaginably wicked, in love with themselves, greedy, and arrogant. They'll reject God, the only one who can save them.

False teachers had apparently targeted women and successfully corrupted some. Paul identifies two who are notorious: Jannes and Jambres.

The Word Is "God-Breathed" (3:10–4:5)

To keep Timothy from discouragement about opposition, Paul reminds him of how much he had suffered in serving Christ and warns that anyone who endeavors to live a godly life will inevitably be persecuted.

In one of the Bible's most important passages on inspiration, Paul confirms that God is the ultimate author of all Scripture, which he declares is inspired by God (literally "God-breathed") and effective for equipping believers "for every good work" (3:16–17).

Christ will return visibly, to judge the living and the dead; Timothy is to faithfully preach the Word on all occasions. Knowing his worldly end is near, Paul passes the mantle of leadership to his "young son."

The Crown of Righteousness (4:6–8)

Paul uses the metaphors of an offering and a race to review his life. While not knowing how the Roman emperor will judge him, he knows that Christ is righteous (just) and will reward him for a life of devoted service.

Appeal and Warning; Preparing for the End (4:9–22)

He asks Timothy to come to Rome and refers to Luke (a doctor; Colossians 4:14), and (John) Mark, who had deserted Paul on the first missionary journey, but now is of great help in the ministry. He also mentions Alexander, who apparently has done him much damage.

Paul was alone at his first hearing before the emperor, but sensed the Lord's presence. He doesn't know what will be the outcome at his present trial, but is confident that if executed, the Lord will bring him safely into his heavenly kingdom.

He asks Timothy to greet some friends and conveys greetings to Timothy from some of the believers in Rome. He concludes with a blessing of grace for all in Ephesus.

Significance

It is reported that on his deathbed Karl Marx declared, "Last words are for fools who have not said enough during their lifetime." He was wrong. Last words often give the wisdom and insight of a lifetime. For this reason 2 Timothy is important. Paul records his final words and reveals what motivated him to a life of service to Christ. The time of "departure" will come for all of us. We want to be able to look back on life and say, with Paul, "I have finished the race, I have kept the faith" (4:7). We want to be ready to meet the Lord.

Titus

Setting

Paul wrote Titus, the third Pastoral Epistle, in the AD mid-60s. Between his first and second imprisonments, he'd preached the gospel on the isle of Crete and started a church.

Of the Cretans, who were notoriously corrupt, one of their own poets wrote, "[They] are always liars, evil beasts, lazy gluttons" (1:12). Titus faced a difficult task. It was essential that the Cretan believers develop a Christlike lifestyle. And, in addition to the integrity issue, Paul was gravely concerned that they were being threatened by false teachers.

After leaving Timothy in Ephesus, Paul and Titus had traveled to Crete. Paul left Titus there and later wrote the letter instructing him to appoint leaders and to teach truth that would help believers live righteous lives. The epistle's authoritative manner and imperative style give a sense of urgency. One of its unique features is the interspersing of three doctrinal sections with personal instructions (1:1–4; 2:11–15; 3:4–7).

Summary

God Who Does Not Lie (1:1–4)

Paul introduces himself and his purpose: He's a slave of God and an apostle of Jesus sent to proclaim the message of eternal life. Eternal life, God's gift to those he has chosen, is received through faith.

Paul emphasizes God's integrity—he absolutely "does not lie" (1:2). Titus is Paul's true son of their common faith.

The Need for Godly Church Leaders (1:5–16)

Titus is to appoint elders; Paul lists their qualifications. Above all they should be blameless, fully devoted to the truth, and capable of teaching truths to others.

The false teachers, or "rebels," claim circumcision is essential for salvation and have led entire households astray. Paul quotes one of their prophets in exposing their greed and corruption and tells Titus to sternly rebuke them. Though they claim to know God, they deny God by the way they live.

Godly Living (2:1–10)

To different groups in the church, Titus is to teach truths that will help them live in such a way that the Christian life appeals to unbelievers. Older men should manifest traits of maturity in their conduct and character. Older women are to act honorably and teach younger women how to excel as a wife and mother. Younger men are to exercise self-control, slaves to obey their owners and be trustworthy. Titus should serve with integrity.

The Moral Power of the Incarnation (2:11–15)

In the second doctrinal section, Paul describes the incarnation's moral power (the appearing of "the grace of God"). Christ gave his life to save us from a godless and sinful life. Because believers await his return, in his strength we should pursue wisdom, righteousness, and devotion to God. These are the truths Paul wants Titus to teach.

God's Kindness and Love (3:1–8)

Paul tells the Cretans how to relate to people outside the church. They're to submit to their rulers and to show courtesy to all people.

In the third doctrinal section, Paul explains why it's essential that believers abandon their former way of life: They had been disobedient, living in sin, but God, in his mercy, saved them, cleansed them, and gave them new life through his Spirit. God graciously declared them righteous and made them heirs of eternal life. It's a "trustworthy saying"—believers should devote themselves to "doing what is good."

Avoid Foolish Talk (3:9–11)

Paul again warns of false teachers purposefully causing dissension in the church. Rather than on godly living, they focus on "foolish controversies and genealogies and arguments and quarrels about the law" that are "unprofitable and useless" (v. 9).

Titus is to warn such people twice; then, if they will not listen, he and the church are to have nothing to do with them. They will be condemned by their own sins.

Future Plans (3:12–15)

Paul explains his future plans and asks Titus to help others who are serving Christ. By devoting themselves to doing good, the Cretans can avoid becoming unproductive.

He closes with greetings from his companions and a blessing for the congregation.

Significance

In contrast to those known as disreputable liars, we needn't doubt anything God says—*he does not lie* (1:2). Like the Cretans, we live in a culture severely deficient in integrity. We cannot excuse our own unreliability, and we must resist the temptation to compromise the truth to get what we want. God wants us to be like Jesus Christ.

Salvation is a gift of God's grace and mercy. We cannot save ourselves by piling up good works. But we should respond to divine grace by living in such a way that life in Christ is appealing to others. It's easy to lapse into useless arguments over insignificant issues. Instead, let us devote ourselves "to doing what is good" (3:8).

Philemon

Setting

Paul wrote Philemon while under house arrest in Rome (AD 61–62). It's one of his four Prison Epistles (with Ephesians, Colossians, and Philippians). Philemon, the primary recipient, likely was a leader (elder) in the Colossian church, which met in his house. He was wealthy enough to own slaves and had a house large enough to host the church.

Paul informed Philemon that Onesimus, a runaway slave, had become a Christian. Apparently, when Onesimus escaped from Philemon, he stole money or property and fled to Rome, hoping to disappear among the masses in the empire's capital. Probably as a result of Paul's ministry, Onesimus trusted Christ as his Savior. Realizing that Philemon was his legal owner, Paul sent him back to Colossae with the letter, encouraging Philemon to welcome him as a fellow believer, not as a slave (vv. 15–16). He also emphasized that Onesimus had become "useful" in serving Christ (v. 11).

Summary

Greeting and Thanks (vv. 1–7)

Paul greets Philemon, Apphia, and Archippus with grace and peace. Apphia probably was the wife of Archippus. Paul offers thanks to God for their faith in the Lord Jesus and their love for all the saints.

On the Basis of Love (vv. 8–19)

Paul makes his request on the basis of love, not his apostolic authority, and informs Philemon that he has become the spiritual father to Onesimus.

As a believer, Onesimus has provided timely help during Paul's imprisonment. Paul wants Philemon to willingly, not grudgingly, welcome Onesimus as a brother in Christ. Paul's hope is that because Onesimus is now a believer, their spiritual bond will transcend the master-slave relationship. He offers to compensate Philemon for damages, but also reminds him that he is indebted to Paul for his trusting Christ as his Savior.

Hope and Plans (vv. 20–25)

As Philemon refreshed the hearts of the saints (v. 7), Paul urges him to refresh his (Paul's) heart by honoring his request. Anticipating his release from house arrest, he asks Philemon to prepare a room for him, sends greetings from Epaphras, Mark, Aristarchus, Demas, and Luke, and concludes with a blessing.

Significance

It has been estimated that there were one million slaves in the first century; slavery was an institution across the empire. Many had become slaves as a result of military conquest; others had sold themselves into bond for economic reasons. In either case, slaves were considered property, not persons. Aristotle called slaves a "living tool."

Beginning with the creation account in Genesis and throughout the Old and New Testaments, the Bible emphasizes the dignity and equality of all people. Though Paul does not directly condemn slavery, he tactfully encourages Philemon to abandon the master-slave relationship and regard Onesimus as a "dear brother" (v. 16).

Paul was an educated Roman citizen, yet he became an advocate for a runaway slave. Like him, some of the anti-slavery movement's greatest champions have been Christians inspired by the Bible.

Hebrews

Setting

One major question about this epistle is authorship. The traditional view is that Paul wrote it, though his name is not given, as it is in his thirteen other canonical letters. The vocabulary and style are different from his; also, the author states that he was not one of those who received the good news directly from Jesus Christ (2:3). Paul did receive the gospel by revelation from Jesus (see Galatians 1:11–12).

Though various individuals have been considered—for example, Luke, Barnabas, Philip, Priscilla, Apollos—the third-century theologian Origen wrote, "Who it was that really wrote the epistle, God only knows."

Fortunately, that question does not affect the letter's authenticity or authority. Hebrews unquestionably is an inspired book of the New Testament.

The original readers were Jews who had made a commitment to become followers of Christ; then, however, due to persecution, some became tempted to return to Judaism. In five passages (2:1–4; 3:7–19; 5:11–6:8; 10:26–39; 12:25–29) the author warns against abandoning Christ and the church. The writer also shows that Christianity is superior, and uses the words *better* and *greater* twelve times to emphasize the supremacy of Christ.

Though classified as an epistle, some believe Hebrews was initially a sermon and then written down as a letter to the recipients.

Summary

In the Past . . . but Now . . . (1:1–3)

In place of the standard epistolary greeting, the writer begins with a statement designed to grab the reader's attention. "In the past God spoke to our ancestors through the prophets at many times and in various ways, but [now] in these last days he has spoken to us by his Son." Jesus is God's supreme revelation, his final Word.

The Superiority of Jesus' Person (1:4–7:17)

To encourage his readers to solidify their commitment and not return to Judaism, the writer gives evidence for why Jesus is superior to the angels, Moses, Joshua, and Aaron. He uses specific Old Testament passages and stories to stress the old system's inadequacy. Interspersed with his arguments are the first three warning passages.

With numerous Old Testament citations the writer demonstrates that Jesus, because of his exalted position as God's Son, is far greater than even the angels.

After warning about the danger of drifting away from faith in Christ, the writer explains why Jesus became a man, a position a little lower than the angels—to die as a sacrifice for sins. Because of his suffering and death, God has exalted his Son, and he has become both the perfect guide to bring people to God and the ideal faithful High Priest.

Jesus exceeds Moses, a faithful servant in God's house, because he is God's Son, the builder and the head of the house. Again, the writer warns about the terrible consequences of hardening their hearts as Israel did when they rebelled in the wilderness.

Though Joshua tried to lead God's people into the Promised Land and rest, they revolted and died in the wilderness. But the writer offers hope. It's still possible for people to enter into "God's rest"—if only they will obey his living and powerful Word.

As Aaron was appointed high priest, God also appointed Jesus, but in a different priestly order—that of Melchizedek. Jesus is a greater high priest because he was sinless and did not need to offer sacrifices for his own sins before he could sacrifice for others.

The third warning passage is difficult. The Hebrews had been believers long enough to be able to teach others; instead they're still spiritually immature and need further instruction. The interpretative problem is that in some sense they've experienced new life in the Spirit, yet it's possible that some may abandon Christ and his sacrifice.

In 7:1–20 the writer explains why Jesus, a high priest in the order of Melchizedek, is superior to the Levites. His argument, which is Jewish and seems odd to many modern readers, is based on Levi's being a descendant of Abraham. That Abraham paid tithes to Melchizedek shows the superiority of Christ's priesthood over that of the Levites.

The Superiority of Jesus' Work (8:1–10:39)

Not only is Jesus himself superior to God's servants who lived in the past, his ministry under the new covenant surpasses the old covenant (the Law). Jesus' ministry was in the heavenly (not the earthly) tabernacle; he has mediated a better covenant; his death on the cross was a better sacrifice.

Jesus is a superior high priest because he ministers in the heavenly rather than the earthly tabernacle, which is only a copy of the heavenly one.

The writer quotes Jeremiah (31:31–34) in favor of the new covenant's superiority. Written on people's hearts rather than tablets of stone, it provides complete and permanent forgiveness of sins. Its enactment is proof that the old covenant is obsolete.

Jesus' sacrifice is superior to the blood of bulls and goats because animal sacrifices only made people ceremonially clean. Jesus' blood provides spiritual cleansing, and he only needed to die once. Under the Law, sacrifices had to be repeated again and again. But after Jesus' sacrifice, he sat down at God's right hand. The work was finished.

A fourth time the writer warns: Anyone who deliberately keeps sinning and shows contempt for Jesus' sacrifice is God's enemy and will be consumed in raging fire.

The Superiority of Faith (11:1–12:29)

After a list of remarkable examples of men and women of faith, the author exhorts his readers to persevere, keeping their eyes on Jesus, accept divine discipline as evidence that they are God's children, and make every effort to live in peace and holiness.

The author gives a final warning that no one who refuses to listen to God's Son will escape God's judgment.

Closing Instructions and Blessing (13:1–25)

The writer gives practical and ethical instructions on how to relate to those in God's family and to outsiders. He encourages them to obey their leaders and to pray for him.

The book ends with a blessing and a greeting from those in Italy (v. 24).

Significance

The primary emphasis of Hebrews is the supremacy of Jesus Christ and the absolute necessity of trusting in him as Savior. He is God's

Son, the glorious revelation of the Father, without equal—the one who made a perfect and all-sufficient sacrifice for sins.

The epistle's recipients wanted Jesus and Moses, Jesus and Aaron, Jesus and the sacrifices—Jesus *and* Judaism. The writer asks, "*Why?*" He shows passionately and persuasively that no person or institution is greater than Christ, who is superior to anyone and anything. To become a believer, we need only Jesus.

Though most Christians today do not struggle with issues of the Law, we face challenges from those who say that faith in Christ alone isn't enough to save us. Hebrews powerfully demonstrates the total sufficiency of Christ's death to atone for our sins.

The epistle also depicts the Christian life as a journey, warning of terrible judgment for those who refuse to persevere in faith. Jesus Christ has blazed a path from earth to heaven. Only by following him will anyone be admitted.

James

Setting

Of the three men named James in the New Testament, James the brother of Jesus is most likely the author of this letter. Though he was not a believer during Jesus' lifetime, the resurrection convinced him that Jesus is God's Son (cf. John 7:3–5; Acts 1:14; 1 Corinthians 15:7). He identifies himself as a totally devoted follower of Christ (1:1), and later he led the church in Jerusalem (Galatians 2:9, 12).

James did not write to a specific church but for a general Christian audience. After the stoning of Stephen (Acts 8:1–3), the Jews launched a vicious campaign of persecution against Christians, forcing many to flee Israel. James symbolically addresses these Jewish Christians, dispersed throughout the empire, as "the twelve tribes scattered among the nations" (James 1:1). He also uses the Greek word *synagogue* for "meeting" or "assembly," and the epistle resembles the Old Testament's Wisdom Literature.

James was a realist. He didn't say "if" but "*whenever* you face trials of many kinds" (1:2); he assumed difficulty as the inevitable outcome of following Christ in a fallen world. Trials aren't necessarily bad. James believed God can use testing to help Christians develop a mature faith, and he urged believers to pray for wisdom to know how to respond in a way that would help them mature rather than sin (1:1–15).

Some trials were external: for instance, unbelievers persecuting believers. Most trials he addressed were internal—issues related to conduct in the Christian community.

James employs powerful, graphic imagery. He compares an immature believer, one lacking faith, to a wave of the sea, "blown and tossed by the wind" (1:6). He tells the rich to "weep and wail" because of their coming judgment for cheating workers out of their wages, and by their luxury and self-indulgence they "have fattened [themselves] in the day of slaughter" (5:1, 5).

Summary

Testing and Temptation (1:2–18)

James identifies himself as a servant of God and of the Lord Jesus Christ.

And then, his opening statement: Life happens. Unforeseen trials are inevitable. Instead of being angry or becoming bitter, believers should rejoice. Why? Because testing produces "endurance," the ability to persevere through troubles, and perseverance leads to "maturity," a more Christlike perspective and character.

When tested, believers should ask God for wisdom—the ability to respond to trials in a way that honors him. Ask with unwavering faith; be certain God will answer.

No one is immune from testing, and all should view trials from the perspective of eternity. The poor and the rich face the same fate. Like a beautiful flower that is scorched by the blazing hot sun, even the wealthy will die. What all should remember is that those who endure trials will receive "the crown of life" (v. 12).

When tested, there are two options. The same set of circumstances that leads to maturity has the potential to entice us to sin.

No one who is tempted should blame God. Though he's in charge, he does not, cannot tempt. God is perfect; he cannot be tempted. The source of temptation is our own evil desires.

James paints a frightening picture of what can happen when a person surrenders to these desires. Like a fish that goes after an artificial lure, lustful desire lures a person into sin that "gives birth to death."

This sort of destructive cycle is not God's will. He is good and gracious. He is unchanging; he wants everyone to know the truth of the gospel and experience new life.

What God Desires (1:19–2:13)

The three godly responses to trials are being quick to hear, slow to speak, and slow to become angry. Responses like these develop the righteous life God wants for us.

Being quick to hear means to actually do what God's Word says, not merely hear it. By responding to the gospel, a person will be cleansed from the filth of sin and be saved.

A person who only hears the Word and does not do what it says is as foolish as a person who looks in a mirror and then immediately forgets what they've seen. The person who allows God's Word to shape them and guide them in life is "blessed."

Two examples of "pure religion," a faith not tainted by the world, are helping others, like "orphans and widows," and not discriminating against the poor in favor of the rich. God has chosen the poor to be rich in faith. It was the rich, not the poor, who were persecuting believers and blaspheming the name of Christ.

The "royal law of Scripture" teaches us to love our neighbor. It is sinful to show favoritism; to break one commandment is to violate the entire law. We will be judged in the same way we have treated others—if we've shown mercy, we will receive mercy, and if not, we will be condemned.

Dead Faith (2:14–26)

James asks questions to show that "faith without deeds" (works) is dead. Faith that does not prove itself in good works is not "saving faith." For what good is it to tell a person who needs clothing and food, "Go in peace; keep warm and well fed," without actually helping them? (2:16). It's possible to believe but not have "saving faith." Even demons believe *in* God, and obviously they aren't saved (v. 19).

James gives two examples from the Old Testament to support his point about faith and works. Abraham's willingness to sacrifice his son Isaac showed genuine faith. He was saved because he "believed God, and it was credited to him as righteousness" (v. 23), but he proved his faith by obeying God. Rahab, the prostitute, proved she believed in God by hiding the spies who came to Jericho before Joshua and the Israelites attacked.

Faith without works is as dead as a body without a spirit.

Slow to Speak (3:1–18)

James explains why we should be "slow to speak." The tongue is the most difficult part of the body to control. This section begins with the example of a teacher, someone who uses their tongue for their profession. Teachers have greater accountability because they can mislead people through falsehood.

Three examples from nature illustrate the tongue's disproportionate power. Though small, it's powerful, like a bit that controls a horse, a rudder that steers a ship, and a spark that can start a raging wildfire. The tongue can be incredibly destructive—it can corrupt a person, setting them on a path leading straight to hell.

The tongue is a powerful force for either good or evil. How can we use it both to praise God and to curse people, created in God's image?

What we need to control the tongue is wisdom. James contrasts two kinds. Worldly wisdom is envious and selfish; it's unspiritual and can even be demonic. But another kind of wisdom, which "comes from heaven" (3:17), is pure, peace-loving, and full of mercy. It does not show favoritism but promotes peace. It produces the kind of righteousness that pleases God.

Slow to Become Angry (4:1–17)

James asks and answers his own questions. Why do believers still fight with one another? First, though redeemed, believers may still be driven by selfish desires. Thus, when they don't get what they want, they kill and covet; they don't pray, and when they do, they ask with selfish motives. Second, they're like adulterers, claiming to love God but still in love with the world. Third, they are proud.

What's the remedy? They must humble themselves before God. If believers will resist the devil, or stand up to him, he will flee. God will exalt the humble.

Malicious criticism of another person is a violation because it usurps the authority of God, who is the only "Lawgiver and Judge" (4:12).

No one knows what will happen in the future, so boasting about what one is going to do today or tomorrow without including God in those plans betrays a foolish arrogance.

Warnings of Future Judgment (5:1–12)

God, "the Lord Almighty" (5:4), will judge rich people who have indulged in a life of luxury by exploiting the helpless poor.

Those who have been exploited should wait patiently, with firm resolve, for the Lord's coming. He will judge those who have unjustly criticized others. Job, blessed by the Lord after patiently suffering devastating loss, is proof of God's compassion and mercy. God will judge those who are not truthful.

The Prayer That Restores (5:13–20)

James uses a series of questions to encourage prayer and worship. For those who are sick (perhaps spiritually weak due to sin), he tells them to summon the elders of the church. Through anointing with oil and prayer, the Lord will restore the sick and forgive their sin. Prayer is a powerful resource for believers. Elijah, by prayer, judged Israel with an extended drought.

If someone strays from the truth, every effort should be made to bring that person back to faith.

Significance

Believers know that trusting Christ as our Savior does not protect us from the kinds of problems everyone endures. Writing to Jewish Christians facing all kinds of trials, James provides guidance for responding to difficult situations in a way that manifests God's righteousness (1:19). His epistle is one of the New Testament's most practical books.

1 Peter

Setting

Peter, "an apostle of Jesus Christ," wrote to encourage God's "chosen people" (2:9) who were despised and persecuted because they had abandoned their former way of life, which involved idolatry and immorality (4:3).

Peter, a leader in the early church (Acts 1:15–16; 2:14; 5:29; 15:7), still referred to himself as a fellow elder and witness of Christ's sufferings (1 Peter 5:1). To encourage ill-treated believers, Peter emphasized the Lord's sufferings. The emphasis on Jesus' sacrificial death is a significant change in Peter's perspective; he was the one who'd confronted Christ when he first announced that his mission would climax in his suffering, death, and resurrection (Matthew 16:21–23), yet in his epistle he uses Christ's example to show how we're to respond to injustice that harms or disadvantages us.

The letter was probably written in AD 62–64. Emperor Nero blamed the Christians for a fire in Rome and launched a campaign of terror against believers. For some reason the attacks were more intense in the provinces of Asia than in Rome.

Peter wrote to encourage believers in those provinces: Pontus, Galatia, Cappadocia, Asia, and Bithynia (in northern Asia Minor). Though some may have suffered physical abuse, the primary attacks were verbal. They were despised, being slandered because of their godly lifestyle (2:11–12).

Summary

Salvation and Suffering (1:1–2:12)

Peter reminds his audience that they have been chosen by God, that they are "aliens" or "foreigners" in the world, and that they've been cleansed by Christ's blood. They are now "the people of God."

Persecution is not a threat to their salvation, an inheritance safeguarded in heaven. Suffering isn't all bad; like fire refines gold, suffering proves and purifies genuine faith.

How are God's people to respond to unjust suffering? First, though in a hostile world, we're "to be holy as God is holy" and to love other believers. Second, we're to grow spiritually. Like newborn babies craving milk, believers should hunger for God's Word. Third, Peter uses Old Testament imagery to identify a believer's status: Because we are "living stones," "a holy priesthood," and God's "chosen people" (2:5, 9), we are to avoid the world's sinful practices.

Respect for Authority (2:13–3:12)

How are believers to live as the people of God in a hostile world? Peter gives guidelines for four relationships: with the state, between masters and slaves, between wives and husbands, and a general admonition for how to live among unbelievers. In the center of the section, he gives the doctrinal motivation for the Christian response to unjust suffering (2:21–25).

By submitting to government authorities, believers are a witness to unbelievers and an honor to God.

Because slavery was widespread in the empire, Peter urges slaves to recognize their owners' authority even if mistreated—such a response pleases God. Peter was not condoning slavery; he was saying that Christians are not to retaliate for personal unjust punishment. Believers are not prohibited from taking action against social injustice.

The reminder of Christ's suffering and death is not merely an example for slaves, but also gives the primary principle for Christian behavior. Believers who have trusted Christ as their Savior are to follow his example. Jesus trusted God and endured suffering patiently when he died as a sacrifice for our sins.

Wives should submit to their husbands, even if they are unbelievers, because by the respect they show, they may convince their husbands to believe. Husbands have a responsibility to love and protect their wives, who are of equal value before God.

Peter concludes the section by exhorting believers to live in harmony with one another and in peace with unbelievers, even those who persecute them. God watches over and hears the prayers of those who do what is right.

The Believer's Response to Persecution (3:13–4:19)

Peter has instructed his readers generally how to live in a hostile world; now he tells how to respond to specific attacks. His words are divided into five subsections.

When persecuted for doing what's right, believers should always be prepared to explain why our hope in Christ makes a difference in the way we respond to unjust suffering (3:13–17).

Again, Peter reminds us that after his suffering and death (in the body), Jesus was made alive in the Spirit (the spiritual realm) and then preached to the imprisoned spirits (possibly fallen angels). In a very difficult passage, Peter compares the waters of baptism to the flood that destroyed the world in the time of Noah (3:18–22).

Though they might suffer physically, Peter warns believers against lapsing back into the sins of their former life (4:1–6).

Though unbelievers will be surprised and offended by the believer's transformed lifestyle, Peter reminds us that everyone will give an account before God. Thus, as the people of God, we should love one another and use our spiritual gifts to serve others, ultimately bringing glory to God through Jesus Christ (4:7–11).

Peter reminds us that we shouldn't be surprised by trials. In a sense, we should rejoice, for persecution is evidence that we belong to Christ and are being transformed by our faith in him (4:12–19).

Exhortations to Elders, Younger Men, and the Church (5:1–11)

Peter exhorts the elders (spiritual leaders) to compassionately care for the church like a shepherd watches over a flock of sheep.

He urges younger men to respect the leadership of the elders and to humble themselves before God.

He admonishes all believers to resist Satan, whom he compares to a vicious lion.

He reminds the church that their circumstances are not unique. Believers everywhere are suffering, yet there is hope. God has called us to share in Christ's eternal glory, and suffering now (on earth) will seem brief compared to our rest and peace in eternity.

Final Greetings (5:12–14)

Peter closes with a reference to Silvanus (Silas), who helped him write the letter, and an encouragement to stand firm in God's grace.

He conveys greetings from the church at "Babylon" (most likely Rome) and from (John) Mark, his son in the faith. Peter hopes his persecuted readers will experience the peace of Christ.

Significance

As those who have been cleansed by the precious blood of Christ (1:18–19), we are God's people. Because we're strangers and aliens in this world, we're expected to abandon sin and live to honor and reflect God in holiness and righteousness (1:15–16).

Though most American believers don't face the kind of hostility that threatened the first-century church, persecution is a harsh and even perilous reality for believers in many parts of today's world. When threatened for our faith in Jesus, we should remember Peter's pastoral encouragement. Persecution does not jeopardize our salvation. Rather, it is evidence of authentic faith—and it is an opportunity to tell others about God's love, about Christ's sacrificial death and resurrection, and about the coming eternal glory.

2 Peter

Setting

The author identifies himself as Simon Peter, one of the Twelve. This is his second letter to his readers (3:1). Though there are significant differences between the two in content and style, the first to which he makes reference probably is 1 Peter.

Peter does not identify his readers, but most likely they're the same audience—Christians in "Pontus, Galatia, Cappadocia, Asia, and Bithynia" (1 Peter 1:1).

After Peter denied the Lord, Jesus forgave him and told him to feed "my lambs" and take care of "my sheep" (John 21:15–17). Peter, a pastor with a shepherd's heart, knew the false teachers were dangerous. They claimed to know the truth but were still trapped in an immoral lifestyle. They denied the saving benefits of Christ's death and scoffed at the promise of his return. He urges believers to protect themselves by growing in the knowledge of the truth and in godliness.

Summary

Keep Growing (1:1–15)

Peter greets his recipients and identifies them as those who have obtained faith and righteousness through Jesus Christ, who is both God and Savior.

Christ has provided everything believers need for life. Because we share in God's moral excellence, he urges us to keep growing in our faith. In what is called "the ladder of faith," he appeals to us to add to our faith: goodness, knowledge, self-control, endurance, godliness, mutual affection, and love.

If we'll keep growing in our faith, we will prove the genuineness of our calling and be honored with a glorious welcome into the eternal kingdom of the Lord Jesus Christ.

Knowing his death was near, Peter was committed to giving an account of what he had previously taught.

Peter's Testimony and the Words of the Prophets (1:16–21)

In contrast to false teaching based on cleverly invented stories, Peter emphasizes that he is an eyewitness of Jesus' transfiguration and that he teaches from the (Old Testament) Scriptures, which were written by Spirit-guided men. The first reference is one of only two in all the Epistles to specific events in the life of Christ. (The other is the Lord's Supper, spoken of in 1 Corinthians 11).

Description and Danger of False Teachers (2:1–22)

False teachers aren't new—just as they had infiltrated God's people in the past, so now false teachers have secretly slipped in among believers. Their teaching is destructive because they deny the Sovereign Lord who bought them. They are immoral and greedy; they'll say anything to exploit their listeners.

He uses three Old Testament examples of God's judgment on the wicked: the angels that sinned, the flood, and Sodom and Gomorrah. Those angels are so dangerous that God has confined them in *Tartarus* (Greek), a place of darkness, until judgment day. Though God destroyed the wicked, he rescued the godly. He didn't confine all angels; he protected Noah and his family; he rescued Lot. The point is that God knows how to deliver the righteous and judge the wicked. The false teachers have disguised themselves as believers but will not escape judgment.

Peter describes false teachers with stories of notorious Old Testament sinners and with graphic illustrations. Though these deceivers claim to know Christ and had escaped slavery to sin, they've turned from Christ and become entangled again in corruption. It would have been better for them had they never known "the way of righteousness" (2:21). Now they're like a dog returning to its own vomit, a pig to wallowing in the mud.

He Is Coming (3:1–13)

Peter, in this, his second letter, tells his readers to remember the teaching and warnings they've received through the prophets and the apostles.

The heretics mock the promise of Christ's return; they are "scoffers" (3:3). They claim the world has always been the same since it was created; in fact, they deliberately forget the world was catastrophically changed when God destroyed it with water. The flood in the time of Noah is evidence that God will intervene in judgment on the ungodly.

Two reasons why Christ has not yet returned: The Lord's concept of time is totally different from ours. One day with the Lord is like a thousand years. And God is patient; he doesn't *want* anyone to miss eternal life in heaven.

But there's a limit to God's patience. The Lord will come unexpectedly, "like a thief" (v. 10). He will destroy the present heavens and earth by fire, and he'll create new heavens and a new earth—a world of perfect righteousness.

While Waiting . . . (3:14–18)

Knowing this, we are to make every effort to be holy and at peace with God. God's patience should motivate people to repent, just as Paul wrote in his letters. Peter admits that some of what Paul wrote is hard to understand, but everything Paul wrote is inspired just as "the other Scriptures"—referring here to the Old Testament.

Peter closes with a warning about being carried away by the error of the lawless and gives encouragement to grow in grace and knowledge of the Lord. His final word is a doxology: "To him be glory both now and forever! Amen" (v. 18).

Significance

Peter emphasizes how important it is for Christians to know what they believe. Believers will always face the threat of godless frauds who distort the truth, are driven by greed, and are trapped in sinful ways. Their judgment is as certain as the Lord's return. We need to know how to distinguish from error and then choose rightly.

1 John

Setting

The apostle John (not John the Baptist) is the author. He and James, his brother, were fishermen who immediately left their nets, their boat, and their father to follow Jesus (Matthew 4:21–22). He was one of Jesus' closest friends, the one whom "Jesus loved" (John 13:23); he wrote the fourth gospel, three epistles, and Revelation.

When the Romans destroyed Jerusalem around AD 70, John left the city and went to Ephesus in western Asia Minor (now western Turkey), where he continued a pastoral ministry to the churches.

Late in the first century, a group who claimed they were believers left the church and started a heretical movement denying that Jesus Christ is God come in the flesh. They rejected John's apostolic authority and tried to convince others to join them. John wrote this letter to expose their false teaching as well as to proclaim what the apostles had seen and heard so that believers might have fellowship with them and with the Father and his Son, Jesus, that their joy might be complete (1:3–4).

An example of the kind of heresy John was refuting comes from the second century. Cerinthius, leader of an early Gnostic group, taught that Jesus was not God's Son, was not virgin born, and that he was a mere man. According to him, Christ was a spirit being, who descended on the man Jesus in the form of a dove, and then left him before his crucifixion so that Christ, a spirit, was untouched by flesh (which Cerinthius said is intrinsically evil).

Summary

The Joy of Fellowship (1:1–4)

Instead of a standard greeting, John begins with a proclamation. He affirms that he and the other apostles witnessed the earthly life of Jesus. He wants believers to enjoy the same fellowship he has with the Father and with his Son, Jesus Christ.

Righteousness, Love, and Belief (1:5–2:29)

John loves his readers like a father loves his children. To help them remain in fellowship with the Lord, John provides his children with three tests: righteousness, love, and belief.

The person who has true fellowship with God will walk in the light because God is light and in him there is no darkness. Believers will realize they are sinners but will not practice sin; when a Christian does sin, he will confess it, knowing that Jesus Christ died as the sacrifice for their sins.

Obedience to God's commands is a second faith test, especially following the command to love. Jesus set a new standard for love, and believers are to love as he did. Anyone who loves the world is not of the Father. The world is an evil, corrupt system destined for destruction.

Many antichrists have come into the world. John identifies an antichrist as anyone who teaches that Jesus is not the Christ and the Son of God. The antichrists have proved themselves false teachers by leaving the church.

They are liars and do not know the truth. In contrast, believers have received the Holy Spirit, who enables them to know the truth and remain in fellowship with Christ.

Righteousness, Love, and Belief (3:1–5:12)

In the epistle's second half, John builds on these "tests" to give believers assurance that they are God's children.

He asks his readers to think about how much God loves them. Because they're destined to be like Christ, they are to keep themselves from sin in anticipation of his visible return. Sinning violates God's law, and anyone who continues in sin does not know Christ. Such a person is a child of the devil.

Christians are to love one another; John gives a negative and then a positive example. He refers first to Cain, who killed his brother, and then to Christ, who gave up his life in unselfish love. Obedience to the command to love is evidence of whether or not one has the Spirit of God.

John introduces the theme of the Spirit of God. It's necessary to test "the spirits" because of false prophets. The true test of the Spirit is the confession that Jesus Christ has come in the flesh. Anyone who denies that Christ is both fully God and fully man is a false prophet and is inspired by a "spirit of falsehood" (4:6), not the Spirit of God.

John gives a second assessment. Anyone who listens to the teaching of the apostles belongs to God; those who reject John's message about Christ do not belong to God.

John focuses on love as the primary characteristic of those who have been born of God. Not only is God light (1:5), God is love (4:8). Sending his Son as a sacrifice for our sins is evidence of how much he loves us, and this should motivate us to love others. Those who love know that God has given them his Spirit, and if they have the Spirit, they will testify that Jesus is the Savior. John applies this test negatively and positively. Anyone who hates another

Christian cannot possibly love God, conversely, true believers will love other believers.

Three evidences of how a person can know they are a child of God are loving God's children (other Christians), obeying God's commands, and believing that Jesus Christ is God's Son. Who can overcome the world? The answer is those who believe Jesus is the Son of God.

John gives tangible testimony of Jesus' true identity as both God and man: the Spirit, the water, and the blood. The person who accepts the Son has eternal life; the one who rejects the Son does not have eternal life.

Christian Assurances and Warning (5:13–21)

John states that what he has written should give Christians assurance that they have eternal life, that God will hear and answer prayer—including prayer for those who sin—and that God's Son will keep them from sin and protect them from the evil one (Satan), and that by knowing the Son they can have fellowship with the one true God.

He ends abruptly with a warning against worshiping idols.

Significance

The apostle John wrote to refute a first-century heresy whose followers claimed they believed in God but not in the Son of God. John said that is impossible. A person cannot claim they believe in God but not in Jesus Christ, his Son. He testified, *I heard him; I saw him; and I literally touched him. I know for certain Jesus was God in the flesh.*

John emphasizes the importance of faithfulness to three crucial truths: believing that Jesus Christ is God's Son who gave his life as a sacrifice for sin, demonstrating a transformed life by purifying oneself from the sins of the world, and loving and remaining in fellowship with other believers.

2 John

Setting

Though the author simply identifies himself as "the elder," most believe he is the apostle John, who also wrote the fourth gospel and 1 John.

John addresses the epistle to a "lady chosen by God" and "her children." Some think these titles refer to a church and its members, others think John had in mind a prominent woman and her children.

Whether a church or an actual person, the problem was that the recipient had unknowingly invited false teachers into her home (or a church that met in homes); John writes to caution her to be more discerning in showing hospitality to strangers.

Summary

John opens with a greeting of grace, mercy, and peace, and commends his readers for remaining faithful to the truth and loving one another; he urges them to continue in both, as God has commanded.

He warns that many false teachers deny the person of Christ. He wants believers to be diligent so they don't wander away from the truth, and they should not invite those who don't believe in Christ into their homes. To do so is to become a partner with them in spreading false teaching.

John says his letter is brief because he hopes to visit them soon; he sends greetings for their chosen sister (either a person or a church).

Significance

John's warning against false teachers should remind us that not everyone who claims to be serving the Lord is honest. We need to love one another and be careful that we don't inadvertently support false teachers.

3 John

Setting

Again, the author calls himself "the elder" and most likely was the apostle John. The letter is addressed to Gaius, a dear friend of John and a faithful church member.

John wrote to warn Gaius about an egotistical elder named Diotrephes, who had spread false rumors about John, refused to support teachers he sent, even excommunicated anyone who tried to help John's disciples.

Summary

John greets Gaius and commends him for his love of the truth. He hopes Gaius is in good health and is grateful for the positive reports he's received about his friend.

Because itinerant teachers depended on hospitality when traveling, John asks Gaius to provide for John's associates in ministry because they are teaching the truth.

John states his displeasure with Diotrephes for abusing his power. He makes it clear that he is a poor example to believers and he intends to call attention to what he is doing—"spreading malicious nonsense"—when he visits the church.

In contrast, Demetrius is well spoken of and practices the truth.

As with 2 John, this third epistle is brief because John hopes to soon see the addressee(s). He closes with a blessing and asks Gaius to greet his friends.

Significance

John's commendation to Gaius for giving hospitality to traveling brothers and sisters who teach the truth is a reminder to all of us who love the truth to help those who serve the Lord.

Jude

Setting

Jude introduces himself as "a brother of James." He was not Jude (Judas) the apostle, and definitely not Judas Iscariot, who betrayed Jesus. James, who wrote the epistle of James, was a half brother to Jesus (Matthew 13:55; Mark 6:3) and leader of the Jerusalem church (Acts 15:13). Jude, then, who wrote this epistle, was also a half brother to Jesus.

The only information we have about Jude comes from this letter. He was a "servant of Jesus Christ," gravely concerned about the threat to believers from false teachers (vv. 3–4), but certain of God's love and the keeping power of Jesus Christ for those he addresses.

Jude writes to warn about this imminent danger, which was so severe that he changed his purpose for writing. Originally he had wanted to write about the blessings of salvation, but instead was compelled to warn his readers about some who had secretly infiltrated the church.

Summary

Greetings and Purpose (vv. 1–4)

After identifying himself, Jude gives assurance to his readers by emphasizing that they have been "called," "loved," and "kept" (v. 1). He greets them with the threefold blessing of mercy, peace, and love.

False teachers have wormed their way into the church. They are godless and immoral. They have denied Jesus Christ.

Description of False Teachers; Warning of Judgment (vv. 5–16)

Jude warns that sin and judgment go hand in hand with three Old Testament examples.

His description of the apostates is graphic. Like unreasoning animals they are controlled by their passions, they reject authority, and they scoff at what they don't understand. They will come under the same condemnation as the notorious rebels Cain, Balaam, and Korah.

Jude uses powerful comparisons from nature to describe their shameful deeds and certain doom. Even Enoch predicted judgment on those who exploit others to gratify their selfish desires.

The Duty of Believers (vv. 17–23)

Jude reminds his readers that the apostles had predicted the coming of ungodly scoffers, and he urges them to protect themselves by helping one another to become mature in their faith, to pray, and to remain steadfast in their love of God.

Because such people are condemned, Jude encourages believers to show mercy and to make every effort to help them escape their sinful ways.

Doxology (vv. 24–25)

Jude closes with one of the most magnificent doxologies in the New Testament, giving praise to God for his attributes and power.

Significance

Because of the danger from false teachers, Jude urges his readers "to contend for the faith" (v. 3). Christians of every generation have the responsibility to defend the truth, which has been passed down all the way from the apostles. This means we should become mature in our faith, keep ourselves in God's love, and show mercy to those who have become trapped in corrupt teaching and an immoral lifestyle.

Though God has judged rebels in the past and will judge those who deny Christ and reject divine authority in the future, believers need not fear. Because we've trusted Jesus as our Savior, we can know that God is able to keep us from falling and to present us into his glorious presence without fault.

As for Jude's inspiring closing statement of praise, the next time you feel overwhelmed by life or simply want to rejoice, read verses 24 and 25 aloud.

Revelation

Setting

Revelation is the Bible's most difficult book to understand. Writing near the end of the first century, John used an imaginative style known as "apocalyptic," which gives a visionary perspective on history that utilizes bizarre symbolism to describe events past, present, and future. Apocalyptic writing also gives "prophetic whackos" an opportunity to let their imaginations run wild and conjure all manner of projections and assertions.

The approach taken here is to recognize the book as a letter written to actual churches in Asia Minor. Though he uses highly symbolic imagery, John describes actual events (past, present, and future). His purpose was to assure persecuted first-century believers and Christians throughout the millennia that the crucified and resurrected Christ is the victorious Lamb of God who will judge Satan and the enemies of God's people and will bring believers to their eternal home.

John wrote to seven churches in Asia (now western Turkey). The imperial cult was part of the Roman religious system, but it wasn't until this point that Emperor Domitian demanded unilateral worship as "god." Throughout the empire, but particularly in the Asian province, Christians were arrested, tortured, and killed for refusing to participate in the cult's idolatry. For many, it seemed as though God had abandoned them.

John wrote to assure them that Jesus Christ, God's Lamb, is alive and triumphant, that God is still on his throne, that Christ will pour out the wrath of God on Satan and his followers, and that he will bring his own faithful followers to their eternal home.

Structure

Before getting into the book's summary, please note three primary structural features.

Revelation usually is identified as the book of Revelation because of its length, yet it is an epistle—a letter written by John to churches. Thus it is important to keep in mind that despite difficult imagery, John was writing about real events. This is not a mythical story about the struggle between good and evil.

Revelation 1:19 basically speaks of the book as having three main sections: "Write, therefore, what you have seen, what is now and what will take place later."

Past (chapter 1)—John's vision of the triumphant Christ

Present (chapters 2–3)—Letters to the seven churches of Asia

Future (chapters 4–22)—John's description of a series of judgments on the earth, the final defeat of Satan, and the new heaven and earth.

John shifts back and forth between scenes on earth and scenes in heaven. For example, in chapter 7 he describes the 144,000 on earth; in chapter 14 he describes the same 144,000 in heaven.

Summary

John's Vision of the Triumphant (1:1–20)

In the introduction John identifies Jesus Christ as the book's source *and* subject.

It was on "the Lord's Day" when John saw a vision of Jesus Christ, the Son of Man, alive and triumphant and standing in the middle of seven lampstands, holding seven stars in his right hand. The lampstands and the stars represent the seven churches; the vision symbolizes his authority and power to protect his church.

Christ's Messages to the Seven Churches (2:1–3:22)

John addresses the seven individual churches in Asia. Beginning with the church at Ephesus and moving clockwise, they are Ephesus, Smyrna, Pergamum, Thyatira, Sardis, Philadelphia, and Laodicea.

Each address follows a general pattern: a description of Christ, a commendation, a complaint and warning, and a concluding exhortation and promise. (Not all features are present in every message.) The description of Christ in each comes from the vision of John recorded in chapter 1.

The letter to the church at Ephesus provides a clear example:

Description of Christ (2:1; cf. 1:12, 16 for the description of Christ)

Commendation (2:2–4)

Complaint (2:5–6)

Promise (2:7)

John's Vision of the Future (4:1–22:5)

THE THRONE OF GOD AND THE LAMB (4:1–5:14)

As a prelude to the judgments that will be unleashed on the earth, John describes a visionary experience that brought him into

God's presence. He sees God seated on his throne (a position of authority) surrounded by angels who are singing "Holy, holy, holy," and twenty-four elders. God is in absolute control of the world and is worthy to receive glory and honor as the creator of all things.

He also sees that God is holding a scroll in his right hand. At first, John is distressed because no one is worthy to open it, but then he is comforted by one of the elders, who says, "Do not weep! See, the Lion of the tribe of Judah, the Root of David, has triumphed. He is able to open the scroll and its seven seals" (5:5).

John identifies the Lion as the Lamb who was slain but is now alive. The scroll contains the judgments about to be unleashed on the earth; because of his death and resurrection, Jesus Christ is authorized to execute the judgments. The twenty-four elders, who previously worshiped God, now worship the Lamb.

Seal, Trumpets, and Bowls (6:1–16:21)

The book's main section describes three sets—seals, trumpets, and bowls—of seven judgments each. The judgments are revealed in chronological sequence, but it's more likely they are to be executed simultaneously or cyclically. Each series provides additional information about the terrors of God's wrath on those who reject the Lamb and persecute his people.

Between the sixth and seventh seal and trumpet judgments, John places interludes that provide more information on the cosmic struggle between God and his enemies. After the first interlude, the judgments resume with the opening of the seventh seal judgment that contains the seven trumpet judgments. There's a second interlude after the sixth trumpet judgment, and then the seventh trumpet judgment is opened, unleashing the seven bowl judgments. Because they're the last series, there's no interlude between the sixth and seventh bowl judgments.

Though the wicked try to hide, there is no escaping God's wrath. The judgments are catastrophic in nature, affecting all of creation. Though afflicted with incredible suffering and death, the wicked refuse to repent, but persist in the worship of demons and their wickedness.

In the first interlude, John describes a scene on earth and then one in heaven. On earth he sees 144,000 people who have been sealed for protection and identifies them as God's people. In heaven he sees a vast multitude from every nation, tribe, and people standing before the throne of God and the Lamb. They've washed their robes "and made them white in the blood of the Lamb" (7:14), symbolizing that they've been cleansed from sin and have overcome death by Christ's sacrifice on the cross.

John describes two scenes in the second interlude—an angel with a small scroll and two witnesses. The angel orders John to eat the scroll, which is sweet to the taste but causes his stomach to turn sour. The scroll symbolizes that the judgments bring sweet victory for God's people but bitter suffering for the wicked.

In the midst of judgment, God sends two witnesses to testify to the wicked. Initially they have power to protect themselves, but after they've completed their ministry, they are seized and murdered. To publicly disgrace them, their bodies are left in the streets of Jerusalem for three and half days. Then God breathes life into his witnesses and takes them to heaven.

After the seventh trumpet, John records a hymn of victory. The twenty-four elders announce that the end is near for the persecutors of God's people.

John reveals that Satan is the power behind this persecution. He is described as a dragon, who attempts to destroy Christ (the woman's son), but God snatches his Son from Satan. Jesus was crucified, but God delivered him from death and enthroned him in heaven.

For his war against God, the dragon forms an evil trinity. He is assisted by the beast out of the sea and the beast out of the earth. Empowered by the dragon, the beast of the sea is fatally wounded but does not die. He forces people to worship the dragon. The beast of the earth works miracles and brands people, marking them as his slaves.

In contrast to havoc on earth, John sees the 144,000 with God's name written on their foreheads, standing with the Lamb on Mount Zion. They have been faithful and are redeemed from the earth.

Prior to the outpouring of the seven bowls of wrath, three angels announce the "eternal gospel" (14:6). God will rescue his people and destroy those who worship the beast. The Son of Man and his angels come with sickles to harvest the earth.

The seven bowls of wrath bring God's judgment to completion. A great multitude of both Old and New Testament believers sing the song of Moses and the song of the Lamb. God's temple is opened, and seven angels come from the temple to pour out the seven bowl judgments. Though the armies of earth, the dragon, and the two beasts attempt to fight, they are decisively defeated in the battle of Armageddon.

BABYLON THE GREAT (17:1–19:10)

John describes the devastating judgment of a godless and totally depraved world system. From God's (heaven's) perspective, this is "the great prostitute," who has seduced people to worship false gods and is "drunk with the blood of God's holy people" (17:4–6).

John describes the end of the same world system again, but from the perspective of earth. From a human perspective, the world is a powerful and lucrative economic system. People mourn the fall of "Babylon the Great" (18:2).

The fall of Babylon brings rejoicing in heaven (19:1–10). The twenty-four elders and a vast host shout praises to God and celebrate victory with a wedding feast, the "wedding supper of the Lamb."

THE TRIUMPHANT RETURN OF THE LAMB (19:11–20:15)

Judgment comes to a dramatic conclusion when Jesus Christ, King of Kings and Lord of Lords, rides at the head of his heavenly army and totally crushes the armies of the world. The two beasts are thrown into a lake of fire, and Satan is bound for a thousand years. At the end of those years, Satan is temporarily freed. He is still determined to overthrow God and leads a great army against God's people. His rebellion is futile. The devil and his followers are cast into the lake of fire forever.

THE NEW JERUSALEM (21:1–22:5)

The final home for believers is the New Jerusalem, a city described as a beautiful bride and the place of eternal blessing. Unlike the wicked city of Babylon, there are no sinners in the New Jerusalem, only those whose names are written in the Lamb's Book of Life. The curse on humanity because of the sin of Adam and Eve is removed, and believers will worship and reign with God and the Lamb forever.

Jesus Is Coming (22:6–21)

John concludes with an angelic assurance of the trustworthiness of his letter, an exhortation for holy living, a warning about changing the message of the book, and a promise from the Lord Jesus that he is returning soon.

Significance

Revelation concludes God's dramatic and incredible plan of redemption. From the disobedience of Adam and Eve, the divine plan will culminate in the Lamb's triumph when he returns as the Lion. Because of his sacrificial death and victorious resurrection, Jesus Christ alone has the authority to judge the earth and rescue his people. As he promised, Jesus is coming again to restore the earth and rule in righteousness. All true believers can be assured they will triumph with him and dwell in God's presence forever.

Dr. William H. Marty (MDiv, Denver Theological Seminary; ThD, Dallas Theological Seminary) is professor of Bible at Moody Bible Institute and has published three books with Bethany House: *The Whole Bible Story, The World of Jesus,* and *The Jesus Story.* He is unique among Bible college professors in that he teaches and writes on both the New and Old Testaments. Dr. Marty lives with his wife in Chicago.

Dr. Boyd Seevers is professor of Old Testament Studies at University of Northwestern in St. Paul, Minnesota. He received his PhD from Trinity Evangelical Divinity School and his ThM from Dallas Theological Seminary. Dr. Seevers lived and studied in Israel for eight years. He has presented papers at numerous national conferences and has published more than one hundred articles. Boyd and his wife, Karen, live near Minneapolis with their four children.

More Bible Resources

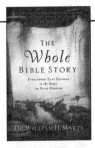

Now you can experience the Bible in one easy-to-read chronological account. All the stories you remember from childhood are part of one grand narrative. It's the page-turning story of God's pursuit of *you*—one you'll want to read again and again.

The Whole Bible Story by Dr. William H. Marty

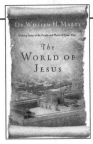

To understand Jesus' life and ministry, we need to understand the history and culture of His world. Here, Dr. William H. Marty provides a narrative history of Israel leading up to Jesus' arrival, and connects that history to passages in the New Testament.

The World of Jesus by Dr. William H. Marty

This guide is for anyone who is unfamiliar with Scripture or intimidated by its scope and size. In *Making Sense of the Bible*, David Whitehead helps readers answer the question "Where do I start?" by connecting them with the stories, people, and major themes of the Bible, book-by-book.

Making Sense of the Bible by David Whitehead

BETHANYHOUSE

Stay up-to-date on your favorite books and authors with our free e-newsletters. Sign up today at bethanyhouse.com.

Find us on Facebook. facebook.com/BHPnonfiction

Follow us on Twitter. @bethany_house